The God Girl Journey

A 30-day guide to a deeper faith

Hayley DiMarco

Revell
a division of Baker Publishing Group
Grand Rapids, Michigan

Hungry Planet

Published by Revell
a division of Baker Publishing Group
P.O. Box 6287, Grand Rapids, MI 49516-6287
www.revellbooks.com

Printed in the United States of America

Library of Congress Cataloging-in-Publication Data is on file at the Library of Congress, Washington, DC.

ISBN 978-0-8007-2067-4

Published in association with Christopher Ferebee, Literary Agent, Corona, California.

13 14 15 16 17 18 19   7 6 5 4 3 2 1

Contents

Contents

Kindness

Goodness

Faithfulness

Gentleness

Self-Control

Introduction

The God Girl is forever on a journey with her Maker, her Father, her Friend. She doesn't walk alone but travels with her forever companion, God, who is the very giver of life and who never leaves her and always protects her. For the God Girl, life is all about him: his will, his mind, his Word. Everything she does is driven by the fact that she wants to love him with all her heart, soul, mind, and strength (see Mark 12:30). She wants what he wants, and she wants what we all want: a life filled with love, joy, and peace. She wants the patience to wait for life to rain down on her, showering her with the gifts of God. She sees that kindness and goodness are part of his nature and therefore knows they must be a part of her nature. All that is found in him, she wants poured into her life.

She has hopes and dreams like every other girl. She sometimes hates the things she does and does the things she hates (see Rom. 7), but she knows that he forgives it all. She is well aware of his kindness toward her in the form of grace, and she embraces it with passion as she daily fights the good fight, though she sometimes stumbles and falls.

But what makes her different from other girls is the Spirit by which she lives. See, the God Girl draws on the life of the Spirit that filled her when she said "I do" to the God of heaven—when she surrendered her life to him and began to see him as ruler of her comings and goings. The God Girl is built to travel this world not alone but in continual contact with her God. **When life seems to be more than she can bear, God is more than she needs.** Of this she is certain.

The God Girl, then, is the girl who knows her life is God's, her plans are God's, and her journey is God's. Because of that she takes her first step each day in his direction. And that is the purpose of this little book: to help you to walk with God on the journey of life. The word *journey* is a good one to describe the walk of the God Girl because **journey refers to traveling on a long and sometimes difficult path of change and growth.** You may have a destination in mind, but it is the journey—the day-by-day progression—that is the life of faith.

This journey that you are on will take you up and it will take you down. There will be days that seem perfect, but just as often, if not more, there will be days of testing and even suffering. The thing you must remember, if you want the pain to count for anything, is that **God's goal isn't to make you happy, it's to make you holy.** Happiness is a cheap goal for life; it implies that your journey should be easy, but that would make it ineffective. Because when life is easy, you have no need for growth or change but much room for distraction and amusement. But spiritual growth, strength, and success are found in the difficulties of life. That's why God can say, "My brothers and sisters, be very happy when you are tested in different ways. You know that such testing of your faith produces endurance. Endure until your testing is over. Then you will be mature and complete, and you won't need anything" (James 1:2–4 GW).

Can you imagine not needing anything but instead being mature and complete? That can be the description of your life, and it will be. In this life you will have trouble, it's guaranteed, but the God Girl can take heart because Christ has overcome the world, and through him she can overcome as well (see John 16:33). When your life is completely identified with the life and the Spirit of Christ, then the world may attack, but you will smile. Your heart will find rest and peace, and your joy will be complete.

So let's take this journey together into the life of faith, into the life of the God Girl. On this 30-day trip you will devote each day to finding out more about God and his presence in your life.

Day 1

Growth Requires Change

Truly, truly, I say to you, unless a grain of wheat falls into the earth and dies, it remains alone; but if it dies, it bears much fruit.

John 12:24

When a seed is planted, it is placed into a deep, dark hole and covered with earth. In this tomb of total darkness, the seed begins to die. It must die in order to grow. As death overtakes the seed, a new life starts to sprout from it. This sprout, knowing it must find the light, struggles upward, piercing the soil and breaking through to the glorious sun. As soon as it finds the sun, it begins to drink of it. It takes that sun and turns it into food, which in turn helps it to reach higher and higher. Over time the rain falls, the seasons change, and the little seed grows into a wispy sapling. As the sapling stretches its branches out to worship

9

the source of its life, it grows stronger and bigger. And over time a mighty tree is formed.

So goes the process of a life developing in complete reliance on a source outside of itself in order to see growth within itself. And so goes the life grown in the Spirit. As a God Girl, your life is the result of a similar death and new birth. The death is rejecting your self in favor of the Father, saying, "I can't do this life on my own. I need a truer source." This is the symbolic burial in the dirt that leads to new life. In faith you put off your old self, which was broken and dirty, and you put on the new self, which lives by the power of the Son through the gift of the Holy Spirit (see Eph. 4:22–23). At the point when you recognized God as Lord of your life (see Rom. 10:9) and stopped trying to do it all on your own, you were given the gift of the Holy Spirit to counsel you, to comfort you, and to help you grow. This is the growth that we will be experiencing over the next 30 days: growth through the power of the Holy Spirit.

The Holy Spirit is the sun to your seed, to your sapling, and to your mighty tree. **No matter where you are in the growth process, you are growing if you are God's.** And part of that growth is change. The seed that does not change does not grow but rots. So it goes that **if God isn't changing you, then he hasn't saved you**. For the God Girl, each day gives the hope of a new sprout, a new leaf, a new branch. And each day of growth makes you more like the image of the risen Christ—that is, each day is a step toward your perfection. And in that perfection is grown the fruit of the Spirit of God who lives in the believer. The fruit of the Spirit is the overflowing nature of the Holy Spirit within you, his very nature pouring out of you into the lives of those around you in the form of love, joy, peace, patience, kindness, goodness, faithfulness, gentleness, and self-control (see Gal. 5:22–23).

Your life, God Girl, was meant to be fruitful, to yield an abundance of that which is the very nature of God

himself. And so it shall be. You are not the same girl today as you were yesterday. And if you are willing to walk on the journey of abundance, then you will produce more fruit than you could possibly consume yourself, and you will yield a harvest big enough to nourish all of those around you. So let's begin this journey together. Let's dive into learning about the fruit of the Spirit and discover how it can overflow in our lives.

Find It

Find the change—Change is an essential part of growth. Whether it's small or big, change happens as God works in your life. But sometimes it can be hard to see God in the stuff of life, so today I want you to consider the past. Look back and find the times when God has intervened in your life. Not sure how to do this? That's okay. It takes some practice. It goes like this: Look back and remember those things that you really wanted but never got to do or have. Then consider what good things you got or did instead. Think about the people who have come into your life too. Can you see God's handprints on them, placing them just where you needed them?

What good came from the path you ended up on? Can you see how God saved you from getting what you wanted?

If you are honest with yourself, you can find at least one point in your life where God did his work and you missed it. But collecting these moments and thanking him for his invisible intervention is the beginning of learning to under-stand how God acts and seeing his hand in your life.

Looking back, what are you glad that you didn't get?

What do you see now was for your best?

Can you see a moment when God intervened in your life and saved you from something bad?

Change is an essential part of growth. Look at your life be-fore and your life now—what change do you see? In what ways are you better today than yesterday?

There is always room for growth, but today we aren't look-ing at where you need to grow, just where you have already grown. Whether the change has been big or small, it's time to take note of the things God has been doing in your life. And thank him for it!

• Pray It

Before we end today, let's take some action of our own, shall we? Take time to pray and consider what you can do today to grow deeper in your faith.

Dear God, thank you for all of the times you have acted in my life. I'm sorry I missed them before, but I'm looking for them now. Thank you for second chances. Thanks for your forgiveness. Thanks for your Son. I love you and I'm looking for you. Amen.

• Look and Listen

Today, make an effort to see the hand of God and to listen to his voice—not his audible voice but the voice that whispers his holy Word into your soul. As he reminds you of a verse you've read, hear his voice. As he reminds you of his commands, listen. As you think of how he wants you to treat others, say thank you to him for speaking. And as he asks you to die to your sin nature and to live through his Spirit, say, "Yes, Lord!"

Look and listen today. See his hand in your daily life. And before you go to sleep at night, write it down.

What did God ask you to do today?

How did he reveal himself to you today?

What Scripture verse did he bring to your mind?

What part of you does he want to die that you might live?

Natural vs. Supernatural

Are you so foolish? Having begun by the Spirit, are you now being perfected by the flesh?

Galatians 3:3

The God Girl is a girl whose life is led by an invisible force: the very Spirit of God himself, who has taken up residence within her body and is guiding her, comforting her, and teaching her to live a life that overflows with the fruit of that Spirit. Without that Spirit there is no God in the girl. But with that Spirit comes everything she needs for a life filled with more than she could ever imagine.

But more often than not, life is less than overflowing.

It's more shallow than deep.

It's more empty than full.

And it's more flesh than Spirit.

When you look at the list of the fruit of the Spirit, found in Galatians 5:22–23, do you see things that are growing in abundance in your life? Are you filled with all nine fruit?

Look at them and think about how much they are evidenced in your life.

Love

Joy

Peace

Patience

Kindness

Goodness

Faithfulness

Gentleness

Self-control

Do you have much of this stuff in your life? Which of these fruit would you say come easiest to you? Are you naturally kind? Do you have a joyful disposition? If so, then you might see a lot of that particular fruit. But what about the fruit you don't have? Why are they lacking? If these are the fruit, or the outpouring, of the life of the Spirit in you, then why don't they *all* grow in you?

That's an important question, because this list isn't reserved for the few, the proud, and the holy. It isn't a list that you can pick and choose from as you wish either. No, it's a list that describes what happens in the life that is led by the power of the Holy Spirit. As an apple seed falls into the ground and begins to sprout, it grows into a tree that must grow apples; that's the kind of tree it is, so that's the kind of fruit it produces. And it's the same with the fruit of the Spirit: the fruit isn't a luxury for the gifted but is a natural product of the Spirit himself within your life.

The trouble comes when we think that this fruit comes from our own efforts or nature. When we think it has to do with who we are, we get into trouble. The truth is that any fruit that comes from your "nature" is the fruit of the flesh, not of the Spirit. **The fruit of the Spirit comes from the Spirit at the expense of the flesh.** That means that if you are kind by nature, then your kindness might just be selfishness in disguise. When you are kind in order to make people like you, to keep them from hurting you, to be accepted, or to get something you want, that is the fruit of the flesh. But the fruit of the Spirit is kind when others are cruel, when kindness is dangerous or unnecessary, because the fruit of the Spirit is meant for God's glory, not for yours. It's meant to lead others to *him*, not to make them like you.

When you try to make yourself fruitful, you fight a losing battle, and that's why a person who grows all nine fruit can seem so rare. It seems impossible simply because you haven't understood that God produces the fruit, not you. He only asks for your surrender, and he'll do the rest. You no longer have to live with just a little bit of fruit, because love, joy, peace, patience, kindness, goodness, faithfulness, gentleness, and self-control can all be yours every day.

God saved you. And God grows you. Allow him to be the source of all the fruit in your life and lean not on your own understanding. Rely on him, and he will give you fruit in abundance.

Verse It

Don't take my word for it. When you are looking for God, when you want to know more of who he is, find out for yourself. The way to do that is by digging into his Word, the Holy Bible. In the pages of Scripture, you will find everything you need to know about him and his plans for your life. **Whatever someone says about matters of the Spirit,**

Scripture must confirm. So get busy looking things up. Find out if the stuff people are telling you is biblical or worldly. Find it in Scripture to know if what they are saying is true or false.

Today, look up God's thoughts on the fruit of the Spirit. Here are a few verses to get you started. Write them down and hide them in your heart. If you don't have a Bible with you, don't worry, just turn to the Verse List in the back of this book and look them up by day.

Galatians 5:22–23

Galatians 3:3

Philippians 1:6

Romans 7:4

• Find It

Take a look at the fruit in your life. Which of the nine fruit of the Spirit come most naturally to you?

Consider your motivation in each of these that naturally appear in your life. Why are they natural to you? Do they exist to protect you from rejection or failure? Do they come from parental training? Do you use them to get what you want (for example, being kind so others will like you)? Explain.

Which of the fruit are the rarest in your life? Why do you think?

• **Pray It**

> *Dear God, thank you for your Spirit and for revealing to me the truth that it isn't by my own strength that I grow the fruit of your Spirit. Amen.*

• **Memorize It**

Memorizing God's Word feeds your soul and prepares your heart to hear him when he speaks. The more you memorize, the more quickly you respond to his voice as well. Deuteronomy 11:18 says, "Take these words of mine to heart and keep them in mind. Write them down, tie them around your wrist, and wear them as headbands as a reminder" (GW). This is God's will: that you learn his Word. So let's spend today working on memorizing the fruit of the Spirit from Galatians 5:

> But the fruit of the Spirit is love, joy, peace, patience, kindness, goodness, faithfulness, gentleness, self-control; against such things there is no law. (Gal. 5:22–23)

An easy way to remember Scripture is to make it into a song. A lot of people have done that already. You can find some of them online, or make them up yourself. Either way, the more you sing them, the quicker the words stick to your memory.

The Purpose of the Fruit

By this my Father is glorified, that you bear much fruit and so prove to be my disciples.

John 15:8 ESV

The God Girl's life is filled with lots of opportunities to show the fruit of the Spirit. That is, you'll meet a lot of difficult people who require your patience, love, and self-control. Much of the problem with difficult people and situations in your life comes from the lack of fruit and the abundance of the flesh. But when the fruit begins to grow in place of the flesh, life sweetens. It becomes less complicated, more effortless. When difficulties hit, the fruit of the Spirit brings out goodness rather than vengeance, fear, or worry. **The fruit of the Spirit calms your soul, turning it toward the life of Christ rather than the life of self.** And that's why the fruit of the Spirit is so necessary to a deeper faith: it points your spirit and others to the life of Christ in you. When the fruit of the Spirit is lacking, the life of Christ is subjected to the desires of your flesh. But as you let him rule as your Lord, as you live to please him and to serve him, your natural desire is to act like him and so to reveal his Spirit to the world that so desperately needs him.

Think about why fruit grows for a sec. Like an apple tree—why does it exist? Does it exist to feed itself fruit? Or to feed those who come to it? That's a ridiculous question, isn't it? It's silly to imagine a tree eating its own fruit. That's not why a tree grows fruit. Sure, some fruit will fall to the ground, rot, and return as nourishment to the soil and so to the roots. But the fruit is mostly meant not for the tree but for the gardener and those around the tree. So it is with the fruit of the Spirit: while it does nourish your life, it more significantly feeds those around you. When you react to life in his Spirit, they are fed his presence. They get to see his fingerprint on your life, evidence of his having saved you and changed you, and so they learn more about him, and they discover his beauty.

The purpose of the life of the God Girl is to bring God glory. Thus the purpose of her fruit is to glorify God, to please him, and to show others how amazing he is. When you lack the fruit in your life, you miss the opportunity to show him off, to share him with others, and to change the world. But when you let his Holy Spirit inform your emotions, your thoughts, and your actions, you become a true disciple of Christ, a witness to his greatness and love. This is what you were made for, this is what you were grown for—to be his hands and feet to a dying world and to guide others to his throne.

The God Girl displays that she is a disciple of Christ not just by going to church, obeying all the rules, and being good but by responding to his voice and allowing his Spirit to inform her decisions and her feelings. Being a true disciple doesn't mean working to be holy or righteous but simply means giving up your life to him, allowing him to determine your steps, your reactions, and your words. When you let the Spirit order your life like this, you will find an abundance of fruit that will feed not only your soul but also the souls of those you love.

Find It

Take a look at the people God has put in your life. Make a list of them, and then consider how the Spirit might feed them fruit through you. Do they bring out your irritability? Then he wants to feed them patience. Do they bring out your anger? Then he wants to feed them love. Do they bring out your love? Then perhaps he wants you to feed them self-control or joy. Look at the people in your life as people who are coming to your tree to eat. Allow God to feed them through you. Pray for the fruit that you are lacking, and be mindful of it throughout the day as you interact with everyone.

Pray It

Dear God, thank you for giving me people to nourish with your fruit. Help me to stop always thinking about myself and to start thinking only about you. Give me a mind that is set on listening to your Holy Spirit and responding to it no matter how difficult the situation. I offer my life to you. I make you Lord of it, and I turn away from my self-interest to live only for what interests you. God, may I love those around me the way you do. Amen.

• Watch It

If you can, get outside today. If not, then just look outside. Find a tree and watch it. Consider how it started, how it grows, and how much effort it put into becoming the tree it is. Where does it get its food? How does it stay alive? Why is it alive? What purpose does the tree serve? Find as many purposes for the tree as you can. How does it serve the animal kingdom, including you? How does it serve itself? And what does a gardener do with a tree that is barren, producing no good thing? Ask God to teach you about the fruit of the Spirit through this exercise. Take a look at these verses as you pray (you can find them in the back of the book).

1 Corinthians 12:7
John 15:4–5
Luke 6:43–44
Matthew 3:10

Day 4

Love

Love Hurts

For if you love those who love you, what reward do you have?
Do not even the tax collectors do the same? And if you greet
only your brothers, what more are you doing than others?
Do not even the Gentiles do the same? You therefore must
be perfect, as your heavenly Father is perfect.

Matthew 5:46–48

You want to be loved. More than anything, you want someone to love you for who you are, forever. Being loved is an amazing feeling and one that we all want. But love can also hurt you. Love someone and you leave your heart open for destruction. Love is a dangerous and risky thing. It exposes you to rejection, to failure, and to pain. And because it's so dangerous, it can be easy to give up on it, or at least to determine to never again give your love to anyone who might not give it in return.

This kind of thinking makes sense to the flesh, but the Spirit has other things in mind. In fact, the Spirit loves those who don't love him back and wants you to do the same thing. While you were a sinner, God loved you (see Rom. 5:8; Eph. 2:4–5). While they crucified Jesus, he loved them. Love hurts the lover, because love is meant for difficult and cruel people, not just easy and loving people. After all, even non-believers can love those who love them back, so what does this kind of love-for-love exchange prove in the life of faith? Nothing! That kind of love comes naturally; it's a transactional love that loves only because it gets love in return.

But true love—the love that God asks for in your life—is a different kind of love altogether. In fact, **the love commanded by God is more than a feeling, and so it's not dependent on what others do or say.** We know this because of the very fact that God *commands* us to love. You cannot command a person to *feel* something. I can't make you feel excited right now. You can't turn on true emotions that easily. Since God commands us to love him, to love others, and to love our enemies, it must mean that he's not commanding a feeling but an action. That means that the Spirit is the source of the strength you need in order to love fearlessly, to love even if love will never be returned, to love in the face of anger and hate, to truly love.

One of the most famous passages on love is found in the book of 1 Corinthians, chapter 13. You must have heard it before. It's read at almost every wedding in the Christian world, and it goes like this:

> Love is patient and kind; love does not envy or boast; it is not arrogant or rude. It does not insist on its own way; it is not irritable or resentful; it does not rejoice at wrongdoing,

but rejoices with the truth. Love bears all things, believes all things, hopes all things, endures all things. Love never ends. (1 Cor. 13:4–8 ESV)

Most young brides believe this is a great passage because it reminds husbands how they should treat their wives, but the truth is that these words aren't meant for others but for you. They are not directed toward those who would love you but are for you to act upon as you love others. And if you notice what they say, you will begin to see a pattern. These words speak to a relationship with an unlovable person. After all, who needs patience—someone dealing with an amazing person or a difficult one? And who needs to be reminded not to be irritable but someone dealing with a trying person?

You must understand what love is and what love isn't in order to find the fruit of the Spirit growing in your life. **Until you know what true love is, you will only be feeling your way through love, and this is not true love but only an amazing emotional reaction to another human being.** God wants you to love not only the lovely but also the unlovable, as he himself has done.

Define It

One of the best things to do when you are studying God's Word is to define the words you are studying. So in the "Define It" section, you will write down what you think the definition of the fruit is (or in some cases its opposite). Then you'll look in the back of the book for our definition. Take a look at it and then put it into your own words in the Reword It section. Doing this simple exercise helps you to not only understand the definition better but also hold on to it longer. As you do this, you are going to see that a lot of words don't mean what you used to think they meant. Finding their real meaning will help you to allow more of the fruit to grow in your life.

Define It: Love

Reword It: Love

• **Verse It**

Whenever you see the "Verse It" section, you are going to look up verses in the Bible that use the word (or a synonym or antonym of the word) in order to help you see how God uses the word and why it is important in the life of faith. If you don't have a Bible with you, you can look up these verses in the back of this book. Write them in the space below here. By writing them you will get them into your brain better.

Luke 6:27–28

Luke 10:27

John 13:35

Ephesians 2:4–5

Ephesians 5:1–2

1 John 4:7–8

• Pray It

Dear God, teach me to love others the way you love me. Give me your Spirit so I won't be afraid to love anyone ever again. Help me to forgive others and to trust you with my heart. Teach me to die to myself and to live for you so that heartache will no longer paralyze my life. Show me that loving others isn't about me but is about you and your will for my life. Father, give me love, true love, that loves even those who don't love me back. Amen.

• Love It Out

Look at 1 Corinthians 13 again. Write down all the things that love does and doesn't do. Pray over these and think about your life and the people in your life. Ask God to help you today to live in this kind of love, knowing that it is impossible for you to do without the help of the Holy Spirit. So listen to him, learn these words found in 1 Corinthians, and spend today working them out in your relationship to others. Each time that you want to reject others in favor of your self, say no, and instead insist on letting the Spirit produce love in you, even at the expense of self.

Love

The Opposite of Love

Do nothing from selfish ambition or conceit, but in humility
count others more significant than yourselves.

Philippians 2:3–4 ESV

*D*o you love the way God loves?

Do you understand what love is?

Do you know what love isn't? Finding out the opposite of love is a great way to learn to love, because a lot
of times we aren't loving like we want to simply because we
are doing the opposite and we don't know it.

So what's the opposite of love?

Did you say hate? If so, you'd be in the majority. But hate
isn't the true opposite of love; it's a *symptom* of its opposite,
but the opposite of love has its foundation in something
entirely different. **The opposite of love is selfishness.** Sur-
prised? That might be because the world doesn't teach us to

think of love as something that is selfless, but that's exactly what love is. Love gives up its life for another. Love cares more for God than for self. Love turns the other cheek; love gives up the right to get even and to win. Love is selfless, not selfish. In fact, selfishness cannot love. It's impossible, because selfishness puts self on the throne of life. Selfishness, by definition, puts self first, and that's not love.

Selfishness puts on others a list of requirements that they must meet before you will love them. This list is born out of self-protection, self-interest, and self-promotion. It is created, even if subconsciously, to protect your life from hurt and pain. But **this obsession with your own wounds ends up diminishing Christ's wounds.** It puts your pain over the pain Jesus felt on the cross and makes life more about you than him. When this happens, what we all tend to do is to make up our own law, our own Bible, that lists everything that others must do in order for us to love them. This unwritten law then becomes the measuring stick for our lives. And when others break our "law," our wrath comes out and our love is withheld. You might not have been aware that you have a law of your own that when broken is punishable by vengeance, bitterness, resentment, or rejection, but if you think about it, you might just start to see that you have had one for a very long time.

As a forgiven child of God, you can no longer allow the sins of others, whether perceived or real, to be an excuse for your sin. But that's just what you do when you react in anything but love. God commands us all to love not only our friends and neighbors but also our enemies. And in this we see that love for all people is essential to the life of faith. When you react in a way that is inconsistent with love—that is, in sin— you say, "Well, she started it!" and you cling to the fact that someone else's sin is your excuse for failing to love the way God wants you to love. But this is no excuse. **You can't give God the "She started it" line and expect forgiveness.** The only way to forgiveness is through confession and repentance. That means fessing up and changing your ways.

If you have not loved the way God loves, don't freak out. God has a way out. His forgiveness covers all of your sin. Just allow yourself to agree with God that you have sinned by not loving, then trust that he has forgiven you and open your heart to change. The Holy Spirit offers you all that you need for true love. If you will just turn to him and tell him that you will stop listening to the flesh and start listening to him, then you will begin to see a shift. Listen to his voice and let it inform how you love from here on out.

Break It

Do you have an unwritten law—a set of rules that you require others to follow in order for you to be happy with them? I used to, but one day I sat down and started to think about how my rules were not a part of God's Word. My rules were things like this: must not disagree with me, must put me first, must not correct me or fix me, must be happy, must want to do what I want to do. Ugh! Sounds ugly now, but I was raised to think of myself first and to think of others as essential to my happiness, meaning that they provided it for me. Don't laugh—I bet you have your own twisted sort of law yourself; you just have to give it some thought. So let's give it a try.

Spend some time today thinking about the things you have decided are grounds for dismissal. In other words, **what do you consider a reason for you to run away from someone?** This might have started as something you vowed to yourself, like, "I will never let anyone hurt me like that again" or "I will never love that kind of person." However it started, you created a law or two for yourself. Ask God to reveal those to you, and then ask him to forgive you for your selfishness and pride and to break your law in favor of his love.

• Pray It

Dear God, forgive me for my selfishness. I want to love the way you love. Help me to give up my list of rules that people must keep for me to love them. Teach me to listen to your Spirit and to love the way you want me to love. Thank you for showing me my sin and for forgiving it as soon as I confess it. I love you, Lord. Amen.

• Forgive Them

God is a God of reconciliation. He wants everyone to stop being enemies and start loving. Today it's time to give up resentment and unforgiveness, especially when it involves a sin against your unwritten law. Take a minute to think about the people in your life who have hurt you. God wants you to forgive them; in fact, he commands it (see Luke 17:3–4). And not only that, but your forgiveness depends on it—that is, if you are unwilling to offer others forgiveness then God promises to withhold it from you (see Matt. 6:14–15). **If they have broken your law rather than any of God's laws, then it isn't your forgiveness they need but your getting over it.** In order to let the fruit of love grow in your life, **you have to let go of the permission you've given yourself to not love**. And forgiving others and getting over their mess-ups is a big part of the process. Forgiveness doesn't mean forgetting, but it does mean that you stop talking about what they did to you and that you stop using it against them. That is not love. **Love doesn't obsess over the sins of others**, so forgive them today and find the love that God wants to give you to show to them.

Love

What Is Love?

By this we know that we love the children of God, when we love God and obey his commandments.

1 John 5:2

Love is something the world has struggled for centuries to define. With so many different people trying to figure it out, the word has become a complicated one. But it isn't meant to be. It can actually be a very simple word when you look at it through the light of God's Word itself. Love is explained in the commandments of God. It is in these commandments that you can learn how to love God over yourself and so to love others the way he loves them. When you simply obey God's commandments, you find yourself loving those around you.

Simple might sound like a stretch when it comes to living out God's Word, but that's only because so many times we try to live it out in our flesh by being determined, strong, or devout. When we do this we fail more times than not because we are trying to achieve with the flesh what God started with his Spirit (see Gal. 3:3). If that could be done, then you'd have some serious bragging rights. You could say, "I'm so holy, look how godly I am," to show the world what hard work you had done in obeying God's Word. But **God doesn't want your boasting; he wants your heart.** When you give him your heart, turning over your will to his and surrendering your plans to him, his Spirit does what you could never do: he teaches your heart obedience. And so he teaches you to love.

See, love isn't something that you can do in the flesh. As we've seen, the motives of your flesh are selfish. So **only those who are filled with the Spirit can truly ever love**, because only those with the Spirit can love selflessly.

"Nonsense!" you say. "There are plenty of nonbelievers who are selfless and love others the way you are talking about."

On the surface, that might seem to be the case. But if you look deeper, you will see selfish motives. Either they love in order to feel good about themselves, to feel happy, and to prove themselves, or they love to somehow save themselves by finding their "purpose." That's oftentimes what believers do too—we love, give, or serve others in order to get God's approval and therefore salvation. But your salvation never depends on what you do. And your love doesn't depend on who you are, but comes from who he is and what he's done. So in order to learn to love, you must learn to give yourself up to him and to allow his Holy Spirit to teach you how to love.

But how do you do that? How do you allow the Holy Spirit to teach you to love? Well, the first thing you do is accept his love. In 1 John 4:19 we see that "We love because he first loved us". You must understand the depth of God's love for you. When you do, then loving his law and therefore his people becomes easy. It's like this: As a child I adored my dad; he was my hero. I thought he was perfect. I was sure he was the smartest and strongest man on earth. I was his kid and he loved me. And because I cherished his love so much, I was never disobedient. I always did what he wanted, because I didn't want to disappoint him. This is the same way that we are able to obey God when we realize how much he loves us. His is the kind of love you never want to disappoint, and out of that love relationship comes a deep desire to live in his will and to bring him happiness. When that is your goal, then loving him back—which includes loving those he asks you to love—becomes easy.

Listening to the life of the Spirit in you becomes easier and easier as you become mindful of him and his thoughts on love. So **it is crucial to devour God's Word and to learn what he means when he says love.** As you see the depth of his love, the love fed by the Holy Spirit will grow in you in abundance.

Discover It

God's love for you is everywhere, but maybe you've missed it. You might have read about it, heard about it, or even seen some of it, but there is so much more waiting for you. Today look at life around you and see God's love. Find his love in his gifts. Find his love in his yeses as well as his nos. As you read the Bible today, look for all the promises of God. See all the acts of God that he has done for you. Look at his beauty as you move through nature, and discover how that beauty reveals his love.

If love is patient and kind and keeps no record of wrongs, can you look at your life and see God's love for you? Think about the ways God has loved you with a 1 Corinthians 13 kind of love, and consider how you will love others.

Pray It

Dear God, thank you for your love, your patience, and your kindness. I adore you and believe you can do no wrong. You are perfect and good, and your love endures forever. I confess that I sometimes forget that it's your love that informs mine. I sometimes make love all about me. I am sorry for that and thankful for your forgiveness. Please teach me today to love others the way you love me. Amen.

Be the Bible

It has been said that you might be the only Bible that some people ever read. That means that your life as you live it in accordance with the Bible will help them to see God in you. Today consider his Word. Study it and ask his Spirit to help you to live it. Know that you can't do it on your own, but that he can and will do it through you. Think about the people in your life, both believers and non-believers, who need a word from God, and consider how you can be—and eventually explain—that word.

Day 7

Joy

To Rejoice Is to Say Something

If God is for us, who can be against us?

Romans 8:31

*J*oy as a fruit of the Spirit isn't just the stuff that makes you happy. It isn't the excitement of a great day or the hope for an exciting tomorrow; joy is a deeper and more penetrating experience for not only you but also those around you. It might seem like semantics, talking about the difference between happiness and joy, but if you look deep enough you will see some important differences.

First of all, happiness relies on circumstances. You get happy when life gets good. When fun stuff happens, happiness joins in. Happiness is the product of the stuff of this world, and it's amazing. Who doesn't love to be happy? But

happiness, unlike joy, disappears when the good is gone and the yucky has arrived. In other words, it's hard to be happy when trials come and life gets unbearable, but joy can live in harsh conditions. How do I know this? Because God's Word says that you are to think of trials as an opportunity for joy (see James 1:2) and that you should, and therefore *can*, rejoice always (1 Thess. 5:16). See, **joy doesn't depend on good times but on a good God.**

Understanding the behavior and the feeling of joy is important if you want to experience it in your life and show it to others so they can see how great your God is. Since joy is a fruit of the Spirit, it is independent of circumstances and totally accessible through the presence of the Holy Spirit in your life. The Spirit assures you that God is in it all—the good, the bad, and the ugly. He assures you he has everything under control and, more than that, he has a plan for everything in your life (see Jer. 29:11). Your joy is fueled by this fact and encouraged by his presence.

Joy is knowing and being mindful of the Holy Spirit's nonstop intercession and accessibility in your life. When you realize that you are never alone and that beyond that, he is actively working in your life, you can sit back and relax in the knowledge that you don't have to live life in your own strength. This is cause for joy! But there are times when it can seem like God has left the building. It can be easy to feel left to your own devices when the world crashes down around you. So how do you rejoice when everything is telling you to scream and cry? The answer is in the action of rejoicing.

See, the rejoicing God gives us access to in all situations isn't a *feeling*; again, if it were, it could not be commanded. But **to rejoice is to *say something*.** It is to celebrate, to give thanks, to appreciate something or someone. As we see in 1 Thessalonians 5:16, we are commanded to "Rejoice always." This is then followed up with the how-tos of rejoicing:

"Pray without ceasing, give thanks in all circumstances; for this is the will of God in Christ Jesus for you. Do not quench the Spirit" (1 Thess. 5:17–18). This prayer, this thanks, this celebrating is focused not on the trial or the suffering but on the blessings of God that come with it. You might have lived through a terrible heartache, but you can still thank God for closing a door that he knew was not the best for you. In every disaster there is an opportunity for rejoicing; if there isn't, then God's Word is wrong. And as believers in this Word and the God who inspired it, we know that isn't true. We all can rejoice always, not because of what's going on around us but because of who is in us. Thank you, God, for your generous gift of the Holy Spirit to point us ever back to you!

Define It: Joy

In the "Define It" space below, write how you would define joy based on what you've read so far. Next, under "Reword It," look at how I define joy in the back of the book, and then write it in your own words. How would you explain it to a friend who didn't know the difference between joy and happiness?

Define It: Joy

Reword It: Joy

• Find It

Today consider the opportunities for joy in your life.

What has God saved you from?

How has God shown himself to you in the past?

What are God's promises for your life? If you aren't sure, then spend some time in his Word today looking at all of the promises he has given you.

• Pray It

Dear God, thank you for access to joy. Thank you that I can celebrate your presence no matter how bad things get. Please show me the things you are doing in my life so I can thank you and rejoice. I pray that I would consider it all pure joy when I face trials of many kinds. Allow me to hear your voice in the hard times and to respond to it rather than the circumstances. Amen.

• Choose It

Today, choose joy by setting your mind on the things of the Spirit rather than the things of the flesh. As you do, try some of these things:

Choose optimism
Smile
Play
Be encouraging
Be thankful
Pray

• Say It

Today is the day to discover the joy of the Holy Spirit. That starts with being thankful. It might sound impossible, but you can find a lot to be thankful for, so make a list of all the good things in your life, both big and small. Write them all out—nothing is too small to thank him for. Then read this list several times today. In fact, read it each morning for the next week, and see if you don't suddenly find access to more joy than you have today.

Day 8

Joy

The Opposite of Joy

Rejoice always.
1 Thessalonians 5:16

One of the biggest enemies of joy in your life might appear to be circumstances, but since joy has nothing to do with circumstances, as we have seen, we have to look a little deeper. The first thing you think of when trying to answer a spiritual question isn't always *the* answer, but there is often something underneath your first answer, and then something underneath your next one. As you peel back the layers, you begin to see the real problem. And once you get to the real problem, you can more accurately and beneficially apply God's Word to the root of the issue.

So the first answer to "What is the opposite of joy?" might be *joylessness*, and that sounds perfect. But what does the joylessness in your life come from—the circumstances of your life, or what you think about those circumstances? Let me save you some time and tell you that it's the second one. **What you think is the bigger enemy of joy than what happens to you**, because your thoughts determine your emotions. So what is at the root of your negative or joyless thoughts about your life? Fear? Worry? Anger? Resentment? It can be any of these. No matter how you react emotionally to those negative thoughts about the bad stuff that happens to you, it all stems from your thoughts on God. A. W. Tozer once said that **what a person thinks of God is the single most important thing about them.** It's true, and it's also the single most important influence on your emotional life. **Your ideas on who God is, his character, will determine how you feel about everything that happens to you and how you treat others.** If you think of God as distant, harsh, and uncaring, then the bad stuff that happens in your life will be the result of either mean people or an evil world, and when that's your interpretation, it's no wonder you are freaked out. Who wants to be under the control of chance or of evil? But that's exactly how you feel if you view God in any way other than how he truly is.

See, if you know God for who he is— always good, perfect, kind, loving, gentle, merciful, all-powerful, and present in your life—then you know that nothing that happens in your life is meant for your destruction but all is for your holiness, because that's his goal: to make you holy. **When you see God as a perfect Father, then you can find joy in**

everything because you are so certain of his goodness and grace toward you. The lack of joy in your life comes, then, from your doubts about God. Now, doubts are normal; we all have them. But the more you doubt, the less joy you have, because joy rests in the knowledge that God can be trusted, period, the end.

We are called believers, but when you allow doubt to fester and to trump your faith, you are no longer a believer but a doubter, and the result of that is a strangulation of the fruit of the Spirit in your life. That's because without his Spirit leading you and speaking to you, you will have no cause for joy. **To continually doubt is to accuse God of not being who he says he is and therefore to walk away from the source of true joy in your life.**

If you want more joy, then you must allow yourself to believe in God more than you currently do. Can you remember the moments in your life when you believed and didn't doubt? Be mindful of those moments more often and you'll find that your doubts, when they come, will be shorter lived because you remember his faithfulness. Even in your doubts, he has all the strength you need. Ask him for it today and find your joy.

Flip It

You defined joy yesterday; now find it's opposite. Look at the definition from the last chapter and write the opposite, or look at the joylessness in your life and explain what it means.

The opposite of joy:

Verse It

Write down two verses on joy. Memorize your favorite.

Peel It

Think about the biggest trial in your life right now. Write it down and then ask God to help you get to the bottom of it. What is the source of your joylessness and fear? Once you answer, ask if there is a deeper source than that, and continue to ask God to peel back the layers until you get to the heart of the problem. Then confess that sin (because it will be a sin) and repent, asking God to give you joy rather than joylessness in this situation.

Change It

Think about the way you express the joy of God. Do you look joyful? Do you sound joyful? Or do you spend more time on the negative? As you talk today, take an inventory. Write down how many times you say something negative and how many times you say something positive. If you don't like your inventory, then work at changing it. How?

- Major on the positive—This isn't a self-help idea but a part of Philippians 4:8.
- Smile more than you usually do.

- Breathe—Sometimes doubt makes you hold your breath. Breathe more and take heart.
- Slow down—Commit to less, and don't let yourself get so busy. Being busy is an easy way to miss out on the joy.
- Look for one good thing in each person you see today and compliment them on it.

• Pray It

Dear God, I am sorry that I have doubted you and not seen you in every situation in my life. Please give me eyes to see your hand moving even in the tough times. May I know you as perfect and all-powerful, being fully aware that you are always present and always acting on my behalf. Amen.

• Tell It

Today find one person to talk about God with. This isn't about getting someone to convert; just talk about an attribute in God's character that you have been thinking about. Not sure? Here is a list of them to explore and to brag on him about:

Omnipresent (always present)	Faithful
	Self-sufficient
Omniscient (all-knowing)	Loving
	Good
Omnipotent (all-powerful)	Wise
	Righteous
Merciful	Sovereign
Kind	Eternal
Just	Patient

Day 9

Joy

The Purpose of Suffering

Count it all joy, my brothers, when you meet trials of various kinds, for you know that the testing of your faith produces steadfastness. And let steadfastness have its full effect, that you may be perfect and complete, lacking in nothing.

James 1:2–4 ESV

*H*ave you ever considered the fact that God's goal isn't your happiness but your holiness? God doesn't set out to make you happy but wants to make you holy, and sometimes he must do that through all kinds of trials. In those instances all happiness may be lost, but God is not concerned because he knows that the symptom of a holy life is pure joy. That is, when you see the purpose of the pain and suffering as testing that is meant to perfect and complete you so that you will be lacking nothing, then **joy comes from wanting the same thing as God**—your perfection. If there were no purpose to all the pain, then you would have something to be angry or depressed about, but knowing that God uses it all to teach you perseverance or steadfastness, which leads to making you complete, is all you need to be set free to a life of joy.

When you can accept God's goodness in your life in the form of testing, you get more than joy added to you—out of that joy comes the fuel for both your service to him and your contentment with your life. The joy that the fruit of the Spirit teaches you to experience energizes you and drives you to want to serve him more. And in this simple discovery of your purpose (service), you can find contentment, and not only that, but when you look at your life though the fruit of joy, you see God working out everything for your good, not your destruction (see Rom. 8:28 and Jer. 29:11).

But joy does more than lead to service and contentment; it also keeps a wrong view of God from becoming a part of your life. You see, when you see things through the Spirit's eyes, you suddenly have no need to complain or to criticize. After all, why would you find fault with God's ways? With his plans for your life? Doesn't the God Girl want only the best for her life, and isn't the best whatever God deems good for her? So then, when you allow the Spirit to color your perception of the world, joy flows out of you and you have no more room for resentment, bitterness, jealousy, or the like. You know that your life is as it should be, and the only path you want to follow is the Lord's.

That isn't to say there will be no suffering in your life, but the suffering will mean something to you. That is, it won't be only to bruise you and break you but will be to smooth you and to remake you into his image. In this way, **through the filter of joy, your pain is redeemed and used for good and not destruction.** Those who don't know the sovereignty and power of God are left victims of the world around them, uncertain why things happen to them. But the God Girl knows nothing happens *to* her so much as *for* her—for her holiness and perfection. Once she sees this she knows that her suffering will be used to comfort another one day. And that makes it all worth it, that she might ultimately serve God with her suffering rather than serve the enemy with her whining and complaining, her fear and her doubt.

Redefine It

You have suffered in your life. Your heart has been broken or your feelings have been hurt. Bad things have happened, and you have missed out on something you wanted in life. Don't let your suffering go to waste a day longer. Today, allow it to be redeemed by God for his service.

What are some major heartaches, trials, or tests in your life?

How might you be able to see God in them? How might he be wanting to redeem them for his service?

Think about your suffering as a tool in God's hands: How could he have meant it for your good? Consider the story of Joseph, told in Genesis 37–50, and how he was able to tell his brothers, "What you meant for evil, God meant for good" (see Gen. 50:20).

● **Ask It**

Is there room for more joy in your life? Ask yourself:

Who or what do I resent in my life?

Is there anyone I am bitter with?

Who am I jealous of? Am I discontent in some area of my life?

What do all of these emotions say about my faith in God and who he is?

How can I reject these feelings in favor of faith?

What does God's Word say about these emotions? (Find some verses in the verse list at the back of the book.)

- **Pray It**

> *Dear God, I have missed it. I've missed the chance to trust you in my trials. I've allowed the bad stuff that has happened in my life to be wasted and not used for good. But today I want to change that. I accept your gift of grace and ask that you show me how I can serve you with my suffering. Amen.*

- **Share It**

Consider who you might share your suffering with. If you haven't let God redeem it and make it for your good, then find someone you can talk to about it. Consider James 5:16, and confess your sins to another righteous person so they can pray for you and God can heal you. Then allow your suffering to be used for good by telling others about how God redeemed it in your life and made it worth something more than the pain.

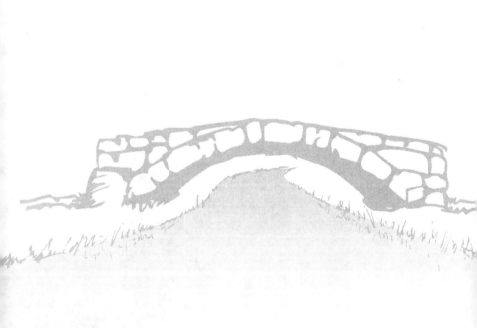

Day 10

Peace

Peace with God

Therefore, since we have been justified by faith, we have peace with God through our Lord Jesus Christ.

Romans 5:1

I am guilty. I was born that way. And it's been downhill from there. I don't do what I want to do. What I do, I hate. I can't seem to get it right. And I am separated from God because of it. It's like my flesh is at war with him, fighting him, pulling away from the gentle call of his Spirit. I really want to do what he wants, but the sin is too tantalizing, too second nature. I, like Paul in Romans 7, cannot resist it. So the war rages inside of me, and the result is a life filled with struggle, worry, fear, and doubt. What I need is peace. It sounds so calm and restful, and so unknown. Peace is freedom from the emotional and spiritual disturbances that come with a life at war with God. And peace is what we all desperately need. With peace you can rest. With peace you can calm your heart and breathe deep. And with peace you can let go of the battle of life, knowing the war is not yours.

But how do you find the peace that passes all understanding (see Phil. 4:7)? The first thing to understand is that **peace, like joy, isn't situational.** Things don't have to be peaceful around you in order for you to be peaceful within. **Peace relies not on circumstances but on the Spirit.** When your spirit is at peace with the Spirit of God, you have found it. You see, **the foundation of peace in your life is peace with God.** Without finding it with him at the foot of the cross, you will never find sustainable peace. The way you find that tranquility of heart and mind is through having a right relationship with him. This means that the battle between you must stop; even the fear of his judgment and condemnation must become a thing of the past.

But what do you do with the guilt? If you believe God is who he says he is and you want more of his peace in your life, then you have to do something with the guilt that unsettles the waters of your life. You must find relief from that guilt, because it is giving your guilt up to Jesus and letting him cover it with his blood that allows you entrance to the serenity of an unaccused life. But sometimes guilt can feel overwhelming. After all, he is a holy God, so how can you possibly accept his love and kindness when you are so filthy? It's a valid question, but if you're asking it, that means you understand the filth of sin. That's good news! It is important to know that **in order to have the peace *of* God, first you must have peace *with* God.** And in order for this to happen, you must first realize your need for forgiveness.

Feelings of guilt are meant to be a sign of the separation between you and God. They aren't meant to doom you to that separation but are designed to lead you to his side. See, guilt is meant to cause a sense of godly sorrow or grief, and this then "produces a repentance that leads to salvation without regret, whereas worldly grief produces death" (2 Cor. 7:10 ESV). When your guilt leads you to repentance and to the realization that you aren't good enough but Jesus is, then it leads you to the saving work of the cross that is peace with God. But if the guilt you feel isn't godly guilt—if it is the false guilt of believing you are too bad for God to forgive—then it will destroy you from the inside out and peace will never be yours. In order to find peace in your life, you must accept the forgiveness of your guilt, all of it, and not hold on to any notion that you are not acceptable to God. His Word promises the removal of all of your guilt and the gift of peace through his Holy Spirit (see Rom. 5:1).

Verse It

Write out the following verses:

1 John 1:9

Romans 8:1

Psalm 32:5

Proverbs 28:13

• Define It

Take a look at these two kinds of guilt, and then put yours into the correct category.

Godly guilt: Guilt felt when you sin against God. This guilt is the result of disobeying God's Word.

Worldly guilt: Guilt you still feel after having confessed your sin to God, or guilt you feel for having done something that wasn't disobedience to God (i.e., guilty feelings associated with disappointing someone, doing something stupid or embarrassing, failure, etc.), or feelings of guilt that drive you away from God out of fear or because you doubt his kindness.

• List It

Which kind of guilt do you have?

Godly guilt in my life:

Worldly guilt in my life:

• Confess It

Peace starts with confession of sin. If you have areas in your life that you cannot let go of, godly guilt that stresses you, worries that plague you, then confess that stuff right now. If it is godly guilt, then you can call your sin a sin and agree with God. Then say, "Thank you for your forgiveness." Make it the practice of your life to confess your sins daily and to trust his forgiveness. If you struggle with this concept, pick a verse on forgiveness, memorize it, and repeat it to yourself every day.

• Get Over It

If the guilt you are feeling is worldly guilt, then you must do the work of letting it go. This starts with the simple realization that it is bad guilt. Identify it, and then let it go!

• Pray It

Dear God, thank you for the forgiveness of all of my sins. I agree that your Word is good and that I am a sinner. But thanks to the blood of your Son, I can be set free from the guilt and so find peace with you. Thank you for setting me free from the bondage of sin and guilt. I love you, Lord. Amen.

Day 11

Peace

The Peace of God

And the peace of God, which surpasses all understanding,
will guard your hearts and your minds in Christ Jesus.

Philippians 4:7

There is nothing more beautiful than peace with God.
It sets you free from all the turmoil and doubt in your
life that weighs heavily on you because of your sinful
nature. And once you accept his forgiveness, the peace of
God becomes yours.

The kind of peace that surpasses all understanding is only
available through the Holy Spirit himself. If you try to gen-
erate peace on your own through making life just like you
want it, you'll fail every time. Even if you try to set the stage
for peace by being diligent to guard and protect it, you will

only have a cheap imitation of peace. Unending peace in all situations isn't generated by human strength, because as long as you're exerting your strength, your body is active, not at rest. There is no self-help book, no relaxation CD, and no exercise that will give you true peace. A soak in a nice bubble bath with candles and soft music might seem like the epitome of peace, but it's just the calm before the storm. That's why so many people say things like, "If life is going good right now, look out, because trouble is on its way." This idea comes from the fact that people try to find peace in circumstances, but knowing that Jesus said, "In this world you will have trouble" (John 16:33 NIV), they see no way around it. And when that trouble comes, the peace based on circumstances hightails it out of town. So they end up just waiting for the other shoe to drop, fearing the chaos that is sure to come after too much serenity in life.

But this is a lie. It's a bald-faced accusation of God, calling him cruel and heartless. **Thinking that peace is fleeting and that chaos is just around the corner assumes a God who loves to toy with you and torture you with the occasional ambush just to keep you on your toes.** Nothing could be further from the truth. God is anything but cruel; he is a loving Father, a kind and merciful God who has only your best interests at heart. But as he said, this life is full of trouble; it's the nature of a sinful world. But right before and after this statement of trouble found in John 16:33 are these words: "I have said these things to you, that in me you may have peace" and "take heart; I have overcome the world" (ESV). This tells us that yes, there will be trouble, but peace is still yours, even in the midst of it, because of who Jesus is—God, the overcomer of this world. So no matter how bad things get, it's all peace, all of the time, to those who take heart in the life of Christ. When you have peace with God, you get the peace of God in your life.

This peace then provides you release from fear of the future and fear of the present. It keeps you from striving to make your life just how you think it ought to be and helps you instead rest on the fact that God makes life just how it should be. The Holy Spirit working in you confirms God's sovereignty in all of life. That means that when times get tough and trouble hits, his voice assures you that all is well and that there is no need to worry because he works everything out for your good. He has plans you can't understand, and if you will allow him to be Lord of your life, he will do with you many great things—things that might involve pain and suffering but that will prove to be for your perfection and peace. The life of Joseph is a great example of this. He went through a lot of turmoil at the hands of his hateful brothers, was sold into slavery, and was put into prison. Yet all this was meant not to destroy him but to save him and his family (see Gen. 37–50). When you have peace with God, you have peace in all situations because you are certain that as a temple of his Holy Spirit, you are forever in his charge and guarded by his mighty hand.

● **Say It**

What are your thoughts on God? How would you describe him as a Father and protector?

How do these thoughts agree with these descriptions of him—kind, loving, trustworthy, faithful, gentle, merciful, generous, righteous, patient, forgiving, and compassionate?

If you have a hard time seeing God as a gentle and trustworthy God, then ask him today to reveal himself to you.

- **Verse It**

    Luke 6:36

    Psalm 57:10

    Lamentations 3:22–24

- **Read It**

    Read the following passage out loud three times:

    > *The LORD is merciful and gracious,*
    > *slow to anger and abounding in steadfast love.*
    > *He will not always chide,*
    > *nor will he keep his anger forever.*
    > *He does not deal with us according to our sins,*
    > *nor repay us according to our iniquities.*
    > *For as high as the heavens are above the earth,*
    > *so great is his steadfast love toward those*
    > *who fear him;*
    > *as far as the east is from the west,*
    > *so far does he remove our transgressions*
    > *from us.*

*As a father shows compassion to his children,
so the LORD shows compassion to those who
fear him. (Ps. 103:8–13)*

What does this mean in your life today?

In what ways have you forgotten or ignored these things about God?

● **Pray It**

*Dear God, thank you for the gift of peace in every situation.
I confess that I sometimes believe that when life gets good,
you are about to make me suffer. I have had a wrong idea of
who you are. Thank you for your kindness, love, and goodness.
I know you are compassionate and merciful, and because of
that you offer me the gift of perfect peace. I accept it today
and ask you to speak it to me in all the situations of my life.
I love you. Amen.*

Day 12

Peace with Others

Beloved, never avenge yourselves, but leave it to the wrath of God, for it is written, "Vengeance is mine, I will repay, says the Lord." To the contrary, "if your enemy is hungry, feed him; if he is thirsty, give him something to drink; for by so doing you will heap burning coals on his head." Do not be overcome by evil, but overcome evil with good.

Romans 12:19–21

One of the first places that peace disappears is in relationship to other people. Disagreements, arguments, rejection, hurt—it all comes out of relationships with people. So how does the fruit of the Spirit called peace exist when people disappoint or frustrate you? How do you live a peaceful life when others are pressing you for a fight? The key is in understanding the source of conflict in your life. It isn't them, it's you. And that's a good thing, because you are powerless to change them, but you can change yourself. So let's see how that works.

Conflict, the opposite of peace, happens when you find a need to protect yourself from something someone else says or does. When you're in the mode of self-protection, peace takes a backseat to the battle, because peace doesn't protect you but leaves you vulnerable to the forces outside of yourself. In this self-protection mode, things like competition, standing up for yourself, and proving yourself take center stage. And in all of these situations, life becomes all about you, and the voice of the Holy Spirit is pushed down and unheard over the cacophony of the flesh.

At the root of this way of thinking is the idea that God can't be trusted to protect you, so you have to do it yourself. This kind of thinking pushes peace out of the picture. After all, peace suggests that Jesus has overcome the world, and clearly he has not, because your life feels like a lonely and stressful struggle on every front. Right?

Wrong.

This is a big mistake. There are no battles for you to fight where God's ultimate victory is in doubt. And while the minutia of your life's future may be unknown to you, knowing God will work your twists and turns together for good is where true peace lies. That fruit of peace is grown in continually returning to the Holy Spirit to ask his direction

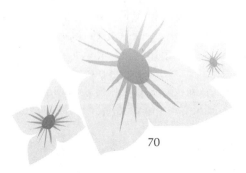

and his will rather than heading out on your own, fighting fights and warding off ambushes. This is not your battle; it is the Lord's (see 1 Sam. 17:47). Peace is meant to be yours, because the only fight to be fought is the good fight of faith. The battle is one of continually returning to the truth that it is through his Spirit, not your power, that lives are changed. This applies just as much to those around you—going to battle with other people does not change them, but it changes you from a faithful one to a doubter, because in the need to prove something, you doubt that God is sufficient, and you fail to trust him. Then peace is gone, and you are left on your own in the struggles of life.

But the Holy Spirit is always there in the life of faith, always waiting for you to turn your ear to him and to trust that no matter what battles rage around you, peace remains. It is the peace the psalmist knew full well as he said, "We will not fear though the earth gives way, though the mountains be moved into the heart of the sea, though its waters roar and foam, though the mountains tremble at its swelling" (Ps. 46:2–3 ESV). And so it goes that the life lived through the filter of the Holy Spirit will find peace, because you have nothing to fear when you trust God with your life, your reputation, and your future.

Think about It

What is at the root of your conflicts with other people? Can you see the places where you fight for self-protection and to prove yourself?

In what ways does this reveal your distrust in God as protector and provider?

In what ways does it reveal you putting your self-interest above God's?

How easily offended are you? What does being offended do to your peace?

Why are you offended by others?

What is an alternative to taking offense?

Are there any conflicts you are entangled in right now? If so, what would God have you do to remove yourself from them? Pray and ask him now.

Matthew 6:14 says, "For if you forgive others their trespasses, your heavenly Father will also forgive you." Is there someone you need to forgive? You don't need to ask their forgiveness unless they are aware of the conflict. If they are unaware, then forgiveness involves you giving up your right to obsess over what they did and deciding not to talk about it with anyone else ever again. In this way you forgive them by not using it against them anymore. When you do this, you will find peace.

Give It

Is there someone in your life who needs the fruit of peace from you? God is a God of peace and reconciliation. If someone has something against you and you are at odds with them, make peace. In this way you will feed them the fruit of the Spirit and allow them to see God in a beautiful and tangible way.

• Pray It

Dear God, teach me to lose. Teach me to put you first and allow myself to be last. I do not know how to die to myself and my fears, but I trust your Holy Spirit to teach me as you give me the peace that passes all understanding. Please allow me to feel the peace that exists even when people anger me, hurt me, or reject me. Amen.

• Lose It

This week, be willing to lose. The next time you are corrected or rejected, be willing to lose, not in order to punish yourself but to experience your trust in God and your devotion to him over your own reputation. Trust him to prove you, to be your voice and your Savior, and give up your right to fight.

Day 13

Patience

What Is Patience?

Rejoice in hope, be patient in tribulation, be constant in prayer.

Romans 12:12

*H*ave you ever wished you could be like God? That you could get people to do whatever you want, whenever you want? You could get them to stop bugging you, interrupting you, or telling you what to do. If you were God you could get slow drivers to put the pedal to the metal. Or you could get things to happen faster, like getting the food to cook faster, the good weather to come sooner, or the computer to work quicker. Ah, control—wouldn't it be amazing? Face it, you've done it before: you've played God, if only in your mind, by deciding what is wrong and right for others, punishing people for their sins, practicing your own flavor of sovereignty. You've yelled at people who irritated you, disobeyed people who ordered you, and judged people who slowed you down. It's human nature; we all have an innate desire to get people to do what we want them to do, when we want them to do it. If they only would, life would be so much easier, wouldn't it?

How many times have you been angry or irritated with another human being and then allowed those feelings to push you to action? In these moments your patience vanishes, you jump into the fray, and life stresses you out. But patience is calm; it is unruffled, at rest, at ease. Sound good? Patience isn't the yucky thing we all think of it as. It can be easy to think of patience as suffering silently, not using your common sense and good judgment but just sitting idly by while stupid people do their stupid stuff. But that's not the real truth about patience. **Patience doesn't suffer; it actually *refuses* to suffer but instead enjoys life with all its twists and turns.**

The secret is that patience accepts every interruption, delay, or inconvenience as an interruption, delay, or inconvenience that comes at the hand of God. Since only the Holy Spirit knows the mind of God (see 1 Cor. 2:11), the Spirit reveals to those who will listen the beautiful truth that God has it all under control, even the difficult people and trying situations of life, and assures you that they are all there in order to make your life more holy, not more miserable.

Your patience, then, reveals to those around you a heart that trusts God with even the minor details. It reveals that you trust him to open the doors he wants open and to shut those he wants shut. Patience is the result of a mind that is totally focused on God and therefore can overlook every trying situation as another stepping-stone on the path of faith. **Patience is your willingness to suffer pain without complaint.** It is trusting your suffering to God and so not needing to voice your concern over it but instead being able to assume the best, since the best is all he gives. When you think like this, and when you respond to the Holy Spirit who confirms this truth in you, you can tolerate any delay that might happen in your life. You can handle things not going the way you imagined them, because you know that God is worth waiting for. So you can feed the fruit of your patience to those around you.

It can be very hard to be patient when others work evil against you and when interruptions threaten the fruit in your life, but patience endures without resentment or bitterness. And because of that, patience soothes your chafing soul; it gives you rest from the frustration and hope for tomorrow, no matter what the delay may be. **Patience trusts God to be God and keeps you from attempting to control the world as if you know best.** Patience is a fruit of the Spirit that wars against the flesh and its desire to play God, and because of that the God Girl accepts it with open arms—because the bottom line is, she wants nothing more than less of her and more of him.

- **Verse It**

    Romans 8:25

    2 Timothy 2:24

    1 Thessalonians 5:14

● Ask It

Who do you know who fits into the categories found in 1 Thessalonians 5:14?

How might you obey God with regard to them all?

Who have you been quarrelsome with?

What do you hope for that you have a hard time waiting patiently for?

What tries your patience the most?

How might God be using these things to teach you, change you, or direct you?

What do you fear the most about being patient?

How is this fear inconsistent with God's will in your life? If you don't know, ask him to show you.

In what ways do you try to play God?

● **Confess It**

After thinking about the ways you try to play God, it is important that you call that what it is: sin. After all, it removes God from the throne of your life and puts you there, making an idol of yourself. You know you aren't God, but you have tried to take from him a lot of things that are his. Now that you know this, it's time to confess. To confess is simply to agree with God that his Word is true and good and that you are a sinner. It can be hard to confess your failure, but you have to realize that God already knows it—confession just allows him to forgive you (see 1 John 1:9). Today, right now, fess up and tell God what you've done, even if it was in ignorance. Agree with him about your sin and then thank him for his forgiveness, because he gives it to you instantaneously.

• Pray It

Dear God, I have avoided praying for patience because I thought it meant I would have to suffer and be tested more. But I am not going to allow my fear to exclude me from your Spirit's moving in my life. I want more of you, so I want more patience. Please allow me to hear your voice and to respond to the call to patience in every area of my life. Amen.

• Look for It

Today, look for opportunities to be patient. When something threatens your peace, apply patience by telling yourself that God sent it for a good purpose. Explore that purpose to find out why God wanted to interrupt you or test you. See if you don't experience joy in this exploration as well. Don't let the world use God's growing of your patience to distract you into fighting a battle that's not yours to fight.

Day 14

℘atience

What Is Impatience?

To set the mind on the flesh is death, but to set the mind on the Spirit is life and peace.

Romans 8:6

Impatience is the outpouring of your interrupted or unfulfilled desires, hopes, and dreams. It is a fruit of the flesh. And it's probably so much a part of your life that you don't even recognize it. But even if you don't recognize it, you live with its symptoms on a daily basis. Your short temper, boredom, resentment, restlessness, nervousness, neuroses, complaining, taking control—they all are gifts of your impatience. So impatience isn't just a minor inconvenience or a personality flaw, but **it's a response to a self-obsessed mind that is more consumed with what you want than with**

what God wants. Ouch! Sorry if that hurt you as much as it
hurt me. I hate my own impatience, and I hate what it says
about my allegiances. You see, I pledge allegiance not to
the flag but to myself most of the time. My allegiance, my
devotion, and my loyalty firmly rest with myself in every
situation when I'm guided by my flesh. There may be times
when I think about others first, but those are only because
deep down I know they will benefit me. And so impatience
smothers my life in self-interest and self-obsession.

**When I set my mind on my flesh, I am impatient be-
cause I have so little power over the world around me.** So
many things can go wrong, and so many people disagree
with me. But in the end, not only do they suffer because of
my unkindness and anger, but I suffer as well because of
the things that impatience does to my mind, emotions, and
body. If you struggle with impatience-based illnesses or sins,
then you know what I'm talking about. **Complaining is the
most obvious sin associated with impatience** and is a sure
sign of a devotion to the flesh that trumps your devotion to
God. Complaining accuses God by criticizing the world in
which he has put you. When you complain, either through
words or sulky actions, your focus is off of God and onto
the things of the flesh, and this, according to God's Word,
leads to death. You might feel that sting of death as you see a
world around you that is out of control and the world within
you that mimics it.

At the root of all the trouble is a desire to take control. This
form of impatience shows up in our nervous and neurotic
actions and emotions. These impatient responses to God's
plans in your life destroy your relationships, make you unbearable to be around, and cloud your emotions, even to
the point of self-hate.

See, most of the time we do what we do in order to get
life under control, and so to ease our minds and our spirits.

But that's the opposite of what happens. While searching for rest, we end up with the trouble of impatience as we build for ourselves more and more requirements that the world around us must meet. So the self-obsessed become the obsessive-compulsive, the quick and efficient become the control freaks, and the worried and fearful become the Debbie Downers of life. But all of this can be reversed if you are willing to see that these are the fruit of impatience and therefore an allegiance to your flesh. Once you have identified this problem, you can choose to walk away from it in favor of the Spirit by simply choosing to set your mind on the things of God. Each time you set your mind on the stuff of the flesh, you suffer, and that suffering builds and builds until it has control of you. But as you reject the flesh and say no to impatience, you retrain your mind to side with God, to identify with him, and ultimately to trust him. The result is a life of patience and calm that can only come through the Spirit himself.

Think about It

In what ways does impatience show up in your life? Consider each of these categories. In what ways are you:

Short-tempered
Prone to complaining
Bored
A control freak
Filled with resentment
Restless
Nervous
Neurotic

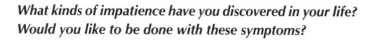

What kinds of impatience have you discovered in your life? Would you like to be done with these symptoms?

What are some ways that you could reject your flesh and so teach it that you will no longer be its slave?

What are some ways you could listen to the Spirit on a regular basis and so get used to his voice? Consider some of the following and make plans to increase these in your life:

Prayer

Bible study

Silence

Praise

Worship

Adoration

• Look for It

Today is the day you look for the opportunity to let God interrupt you. Today is the day to let go of your plans and embrace his. Look for those chances to die to yourself by allowing God's plans to interrupt your own.

• Pray It

Dear God, thank you for being in control of my life. Thank you that I don't have to be. And thank you for giving me your Spirit who confirms that in my heart. I know you are sovereign and in control; please teach me how to act on that knowledge. Give me wisdom and give me patience as I wait for you in every situation in my life. Amen.

• Give It Up

Today, give it up—give up control. Find one place in your life where you are playing God and trying to control the world around you, and give it up to God. Lay it on the altar and run a dagger through it. Turn your life over to him without any strings attached. And trust him to make more of it than you ever could. Write down today your promise to God.

Day 15

Patience

Finding Patience

A fool gives full vent to his spirit, but a wise man quietly holds it back.

Proverbs 29:11 ESV

You can fake a lot of fruitfulness. You can pretend to love, you can act kind, and you can claim to be faithful. But you can't fake patience; the minute you lose it, it shows on your face. The minute someone frustrates you by doing something you didn't want them to do, you explode inside, and hiding that kind of turmoil is impossible. It comes out in your facial expressions, your words, and your actions. Even if the world around you doesn't notice your impatience, your body experiences it, and this experience of impatience gives birth to all kinds of negative emotions that can war within you. **Impatience expressed is outwardly volatile, and impatience bottled up is inwardly destructive.** That's why faking patience is so destructive. But impatience doesn't have to be your downfall. There is a patience in the life of faith that isn't forced or even faked, and this is a supernatural patience that seeps into your life from the moment you allow the Holy Spirit to be your scheduler and prioritizer.

Patience comes to the person who doesn't give full vent to their spirit but instead holds it back in favor of God's Spirit. This shows up in a couple of areas that you might never have thought of exposing to the Spirit's planning. One of those is in your talking. You're a girl, so I know that talking probably comes naturally to you, especially when you are with friends or people you trust. But talking can become destructive when you serve your desire for communication rather than serving the Spirit. That happens when you believe that giving voice to all of your feelings and concerns is important, if not essential. When you fail to look at your words as a medium by which you feed the fruit of the Spirit to those around you, you can misuse those words for yourself. When that happens, **impatience expresses itself in the habit of talking too much**.

But holding back your words, though it's counterintuitive, is a good practice in growing the fruit of the Spirit instead of the fruit of the flesh. In this process you are learning to put God's thoughts over your own. After all, it's hard to hear God when you are talking, and so it is hard to respond to his Spirit while your mouth is moving. You could say that your patience with others starts with your patience with God: giving him the time to speak by spending time in his Word, and giving yourself time to understand what feeds the fruit of patience in your life.

Another way for you to encourage the growth of patience in your life is to stand back and look at what really matters. Most of the stuff that makes you blow your stack is inconsequential in the grand scheme of things. But telling yourself that in the middle of your impatience is ineffective. The better plan is to start to prioritize your life. Decide what's the most important thing in the world, and then go from there. If you are a God Girl, then I can tell you that the most important thing is God and his plan. But if you prioritize those things that aren't as important as God as, well, not as important as God and his plan, when those less important things get interrupted, you won't feel the need to freak out like you used to. When you understand God's sovereignty (his complete control), you will begin to see interruptions as coming from him and not someone or something else. So if you prioritize blogging or texting as less important than loving God and giving him the glory, then when you are interrupted while blogging, you won't freak, because you've given it less importance than you used to.

Prioritizing your to-do list gives you more time as well. If you subconsciously believe that the ten things you have to do today are all equally important, then when you are tested, you are going to flip out. But if you have prioritized the three most important things and given yourself permission not to get the rest done, then patience will come much easier.

It all has to do with making the things of the Spirit more important than the things of your flesh. As you do this, the fruit of patience will have room to grow and to flourish in your life.

Prioritize It

Start today to consider what are the most important things in your life. Consider the stuff that stresses you out, and ask yourself what place those things should be in. I used to freak out when my space was a mess, which was all the time. But then one day I prioritized my time with God, family, and friends as more important, and so when left with the choice between a higher priority and cleaning, I was able to say no to cleaning and not freak out that I couldn't get it all done. Give it a try. If there is someone in authority over you, you might want to ask their opinion on this list as well, since they have the right to tell you what to do and when to do it. Conferring with them increases your chance of rejecting your flesh and embracing the Spirit.

Shut It

If you can, decide not to talk today or some day this week. Shut your mouth and either write what needs to be said or speak only when spoken to. Notice, and then write down here, how your life changes when you listen more than you speak.

Pray It

Dear God, teach me your ways. Give me your thoughts so that I can know what is important and what isn't. I want patience. I want to see it in my life for others and to get my priorities straight. Please help me to prioritize my life according to your will. Amen.

• Accept It

A lot of times those moments that test your patience are meant to teach you to be more like Christ. When those tests come, resist the urge to argue or defend. Instead, allow the people in your life who make you frustrated to be a mirror held up by God showing you the areas in your life where you need to resist the flesh and side with the Spirit. Don't be afraid to die to yourself, to be wrong, or to be accused, rejected, or corrected—just look at it as a chance for your life to become less about you and more about him. Today, don't argue. Refuse to let your impatience with people define you, but let the Holy Spirit be your leader and your guide.

Day 16

Kindness

What Is Kindness?

But God, being rich in mercy, because of the great love with which he loved us, even when we were dead in our trespasses, made us alive together with Christ—by grace you have been saved.

Ephesians 2:4–5

Kindness is an often-misunderstood concept. It's usually thought of as a synonym to niceness. But kindness isn't about being a nice person. There are lots of really nice people in the world who know nothing about the Holy Spirit. In fact, you don't have to have the Holy Spirit in order to be nice to people. No, kindness is much deeper than that and much more challenging to human nature. That's because kindness is a synonym for grace, not niceness. Most people are nice to people they believe deserve their niceness or because being nice makes them feel good. But kindness is based on the idea that though they don't deserve it—and worse yet, they may even deserve the opposite—you are going to serve them what God has served you, and that's grace overflowing.

This is the key: **kindness is an imitation of God.** You can't take God's grace in the face of your failure and sin and then turn around and fail to give grace to others. That's called hypocrisy. But as a girl who has been given much grace, you are free to give much in return, and in that grace or kindness that you share with others, you offer the same things that have been given you. You offer compassion, mercy, sympathy, forgiveness, and generosity. That means that kindness is really something offered to people who are not giving you kindness in return. It's for people who irritate you, hurt you, or even hate you, because it is the offering of God's grace in the face of their failure. Being kind to those you love isn't a bad thing, but it doesn't require the fruit of the Spirit, because it counts on their kindness in return. But **the fruit of the Spirit called kindness is born in struggle and difficulty through the power of the Spirit**. The Spirit gives you access to the kindness of God so that you might share it with those in need who don't want to return it or aren't equipped to. So kindness means being slow to anger in the face of anger-building situations. It means being hospitable to strangers, which means people who can do nothing for you. And it means being tenderhearted to those who don't deserve your mercy or compassion.

How will they know you are a God Girl? By your love! And how do you love the way God loves? By loving the unlovable. Unbelievers love those who love them back, so just showing that type of concern for others doesn't honor God; it only confirms human nature. But when you are kind to the ugly and the mean, then you point people to the life of Christ in you. Then you feed them the fruit of the Spirit and reveal to them that there is more to this life than meets the eye, and there is an unseen force at work in your very nature, remaking you into his likeness.

Many people do absolutely deserve your wrath. They deserve to be taught a lesson, to be hurt like they hurt you, but kindness doesn't give people what they deserve, because that would be inconsistent with the grace of God. If you want to lead others to Christ—if you want them to experience the love, joy, peace, and patience that you have experienced from knowing him—then you must refuse the opportunity to hurt them for hurting you. Instead, you must do something crazy and give them the kindness they do not deserve. When you do, the fruit of the Spirit will not only feed them but also feed you as it reminds you of the undeserved kindness you first received from God.

Describe It

Look again at what you just read and pull out everything you can that describes kindness. Think about what it means to be kind as an action, not just a feeling. Then look at your behavior toward difficult people in this light. Are you offering biblical kindness to others, or do you need some more Holy Spirit help?

Ask Yourself

Colossians 3:17 says, "Whatever you do, whether in word or deed, do it all in the name of the Lord Jesus, giving thanks to God the Father through him" (NIV). Ask yourself if this is true of your relationships with difficult people. Do you do it all in the name of Jesus? What do you think that means?

Think about your kindness. Spend some time considering who you are kind to and how much kindness you reserve from giving to those you don't like. Then ask yourself why you withhold it. Are your motives selfish? If so, confess your unkindness to God and ask him to give you the opportunity for change.

What are some ways you can be kind to the people you see every week?

• Pray It

Dear God, teach me your grace and mercy. Give me an understanding of your kindness to those who don't deserve it. Help me to mimic you by giving others more than they deserve. Amen.

• Practice It

As you go out into the world today, find someone to be kind to and show God's grace. It doesn't take much; it just requires a heart for the hurting. Smile at the angry person; ask the unfriendly sales clerk about their day; care for the waiter who serves you. Ask a stranger their name and make a new acquaintance. Find a chance to give grace and mercy to those who you really want to get even with for their unkindness, and share the fruit of the Spirit with those who desperately need it.

Day 17

Kindness

Kindness Killers

No matter who you are, if you judge anyone, you have no excuse. When you judge another person, you condemn yourself, since you, the judge, do the same things.

Romans 2:1 GW

*T*here is nothing more lethal to the fruit of the Spirit called kindness than your sense of justice. I can hear you now saying, "Be kind? I should be kind while they are being mean? Shouldn't I teach them a lesson?" That would be a good choice if you were, oh, I don't know, say, God! But as someone who isn't God, I can testify that it can't be done. You can't teach them a lesson by mimicking their sin. But that's just what your messed-up sense of justice would have you do. This idea that when someone sins they need to be punished gets you into the kind of trouble you want for them, because you end up guilty of the same stuff that you are judging them for.

It is true that injustice deserves judgment, but if you declare yourself the judge, you're taking God's job into your own hands again. And we know how that plays out. But what happens when you refuse to give kindness to those who hurt you? **When you harden your heart to the sinful condition of others by judging it, mocking it, or punishing it, you simultaneously harden your heart to God.** See, their sin is no different than yours. We are all in the same swamp of sin, surrounded by it and stuck in it, unable to get ourselves out. So when you judge them for their swampy nature, you condemn yourself because you're in the same exact swamp.

You can't let your sense of justice, of wrong and right, seem like permission to sin and to withhold kindness from them; if you do, you are no better than those you judge. That means that you cannot hold a grudge against another human being. Holding a grudge is refusing to offer the grace you have been given. When you are unsympathetic to their sinful nature, you are acting on your flesh and encouraging it to rise above the Spirit and guide your life. This all starts at the moment you take offense at someone's actions. When you judge their actions as harmful or hateful toward you, the wheels start turning and you give yourself permission to "fix" the situation. In this attempt to stand up for yourself and to argue against their offense, you close your ears to the voice of the Spirit in your life. With less of him there is more of you, and that more of you feeds more sin and more suffering in your life and the lives of those around you.

But kindness doesn't need to be killed in an attempt to balance the scales or to teach a lesson. Your way of thinking must change from considering the scales unbalanced to seeing how balanced they are. That is to say, **you must begin to be honest with yourself about your own sin and not consider others any worse than you, just different.** Then realize that the lesson that needs to be learned here isn't for them but for you. Each time someone offends you, it is an opportunity to respond to the Holy Spirit instead of your flesh, and so to teach your flesh to shut up and quit ruling your life.

Kindness does more than feed the person who deserves your wrath: it softens your heart to the promptings of the Spirit and gives you more of him in your life. Kindness is an attribute of God, so you can be sure of its goodness. If kindness doesn't come easily to you, then allow today to be the day that God reveals his kindness to you as he shows you that life doesn't have to be the battle you've made it out to be. Accept the fruit of kindness in your life and be set free from the chains of judgment and strife.

• Confront It

Do you have a fear of rejection?
Do you easily hold a grudge?
Are you easily offended?
Do you have a hard time being grateful?

If you said yes to any of these, then kindness doesn't come easily for you. Spend some time today thinking about how your answers to these questions might change in light of God's kindness to you. How can you embrace kindness and get over your sense of justice?

Sarcasm is an opportunity for unkindness in disguise. Think about your life and your tongue. Are you prone to sarcasm? If so, confess it to God and ask him to give you more of his kindness.

Pray It

Dear God, I'm prone to judge others and to give kindness based on merit. But I don't want to be like that anymore; I want to be like you. Teach me how to give up my sense of justice, to trust you with judgment, and to give myself fully to kindness instead. Amen.

Surrender It

Your own wounds sometimes keep you from being kind to others. Do you have any wounds that you haven't let God heal? If so, turn those over to him and tell him that the wounds of Christ on the cross are more important than yours. Keeping them does you no good. They are only useful once they are healed by his blood. When this happens, the scars from your wounds can serve others as an example of his kindness to you. Give up your wounds today and thank Jesus for his healing wounds.

Day 18

Kindness

Become a Grace Giver

Do not say, "I will repay evil";
wait for the LORD, and he will deliver you.

Proverbs 20:22

When you want more of the fruit of kindness in your life, you become a grace giver. You reject mercilessness and punishment in favor of loving-kindness. But what does that look like in your life? How does kindness manifest itself, and how can you move in the direction of being a grace giver?

The key is to give up your sense of justice, and you do that by letting go of the need to manage the situation and to fix the offender. There is in all of us a natural distaste for sin. We don't like it when we see it and we want to eradicate it, or at the very least to punish it. We understand within our very fiber that bad stuff deserves something bad in return. And while this is true, justice is not our job but God's. He wields the payment for sin as well as the release from it. But since we don't often get to see God's judgment in action, we feel compelled to take matters into our own hands, so when someone says something mean, we fight back. When she hurts us, we plot and plan to hurt her back. We believe the lie that vengeance is sweet. But the truth is that vengeance is not only bitter, it's sinful. It is taking something that we have actually heard God say belongs to him: "Vengeance is mine, I will repay, says the Lord" (Rom. 12:19). When we refuse to give grace because we don't believe someone deserves it, we do that out of a desire for vengeance.

Each time you refuse to get over the sin of another, it's out of this desire for justice. Even the stuff you do to yourself that you can't get over brings with it a sense of punishment. But **failing to get over the offenses of another or your own sins makes sin about you rather than about God.** But all sin is an offense against God, not you, as David put it when he confessed his sin: "Against you, you only, have I sinned and done what is evil in your sight, so that you may be justified in your words and blameless in your judgment" (Ps. 51:4). Kindness is choked out of us by this fact that we want more justice than we are seeing.

Kindness does not seek to punish anyone but instead leaves that to God. In its grace and mercy, it gives others more than they deserve, without keeping any account. It's another part of human nature to take notes. We like to keep a mental image of all of the failures of another to be used against them in the future. But kindness destroys the records. Just like God has removed your transgressions and sins from your record by his grace found in the death and resurrection of Christ, so the kindness that grows from his Holy Spirit in you does the same thing. This cannot be done in human strength, and that's why so many people fail at true kindness. You cannot rely on your strength or your flesh to do this, but you have to trust God to give you the ability and the desire. I know this because I read it in the Bible, which says, "For it is God who works in you, both to will and to work for his good pleasure" (Phil. 2:13). This is an incredible thought. It means that God is at work right now revealing both his will and the power for you to be kind to those who don't deserve it.

So whether you've been kind in the past or not is irrelevant. All that matters is that you trust the Holy Spirit not only to give you the ability to be kind but also to give you the will to want it.

Practice It

Part of kindness is freely offering apology. Today, apologize quickly. As you apologize, those who feel wronged will be nourished by the fruit of kindness.

Think about the people in your life who could use an apology from you. Is there someone who holds something against you, resents you, or is mad at you? Can you apologize to them today? Ask God to give you the grace to say, "I'm sorry."

Who in your life bugs you the most when they make a mistake? Kindness allows others to be wrong without fighting or arguing or proving rightness. Think about that person and pray for your kindness with them. Why are they less likely to get it from you? How does God want you to act the next time they do something wrong?

Get Over It

Is there something in your past that makes you sick to think about it? If there is, then it's something that you haven't gotten over. And if it involves another person, then it involves your kindness. It's hard to offer grace to someone who has caused you pain that you can't get over. Look at that situation through the light of the Holy Spirit. How does he want you to react to it? To treat them? To think about them? Spend some time today looking at life through his eyes instead of your own.

Can you pray for the person who hurt you? If there is someone you can't bring yourself to pray for, then you have been withholding the fruit of kindness. Offer them the grace of your prayers. Today pray for them, their relationship with God, and their freedom from sin. Ask God how to pray for them and then intercede on their part. As you do, your feelings for them will soften.

Pray It

Dear God, I confess my failure to let you be the judge and jury. I am prone to judgment and criticism, not grace and forgiveness. Help me to be more like you and to offer grace and mercy freely to those who need it from me. Amen.

Day 19

Goodness

What Is Goodness?

God is light; in him there is no darkness at all. If we claim
to have fellowship with him and yet walk in the darkness,
we lie and do not live out the truth.

1 John 1:5–6 NIV

What is good?
Who decided?
How do you define goodness in your life? Goodness can be a hard term to understand because what's good for one person might not be good for another. That's why a lot of people have decided that goodness is subjective, different for everyone, and everyone can make up their own mind about what is good for them. But when that's your way of figuring out what goodness is, your goodness can

quickly become someone else's sadness. When what's good for you hurts someone else, then defining goodness based on your own opinion becomes dangerous. True goodness isn't subjective but definable. That's because it's been defined by goodness himself—God.

When and only when you want what God wants do you find goodness. All other attempts at defining what is good for you are going to fail because they carry with them your doubt about God's own goodness and his right to define it for your life. When you argue with God over what's good, or when you think something that he has defined as evil is good, then you are faced with a spiritual rebellion against the Holy Spirit, and you end up in the dark. In this darkness you hide and you cower in shame, like Adam and Eve after the bite of the apple. You feel empty and alone, dark and dirty.

But goodness doesn't live in darkness; it lives in the light. And in the light there is freedom, peace, and strength. In the light your life feels right, clean, safe, and good. In any understanding of what goodness is you have to know that goodness is defined by what God deems good. And you can know what God considers good by looking at his Word. In the Bible he has written all that he deemed necessary to teach you what is good to him. **All the commands of Scripture are a definition of goodness for the life of the God Girl.** Goodness is seen in a love of those commands—not a fear of punishment but a love for whatever he loves. This is the essence of goodness: loving what God loves. That's why Ephesians 5:10 tells us to "find out what pleases the Lord" (NIV), not in order to be saved, because only your faith in Jesus can do that, but in order to discover true goodness. After all, how can you please someone if you don't know what's good to them? The healthy desire to please another comes from your love for them, not your fear of losing them. So goodness comes from your love for God, not your fear of losing your salvation. Goodness isn't about being good to gain God's love but being good because God is good and his Spirit teaches you goodness.

Goodness lives in the light because that's where God is. As you bring your life into the light, you not only get a better look at the areas where you have rejected goodness, but you also find the opportunity to get rid of the darkness that plagues you. The light of God not only exposes sin but cleanses it. It does that by giving you the opportunity to spot it. Sin is at the root of all of your struggles, so turning the lights on so you can see the sin that's underneath the pain gives you the chance to get rid of the sin by confession. Coming into the light offers you the chance to be free from the stuff that plagues you and to choose goodness. You cannot live in darkness and have fellowship with God. You have to let him expose your life to the light, and then you will find all the goodness you are lacking.

Confess It

First John 1:10 says, "If we say we have not sinned, we make him a liar, and his word is not in us." That's because we all sin, every single one of us. Darkness comes when you say you have no sin in your life. But living in the light brings out all the sin in order to get rid of it. Where is there darkness in your life, some area that you don't want exposed to the light? Do you think the darkness hides you from God? Not so (see Ps. 139:11–12). Today, turn on the lights. If you are not sure how, here are some ideas.

Pray—Give God access to your life. Ask him to shine the light of Jesus on all of it and show you the areas of sin that you have been hiding.

Avoid the darkness—If there are people in your life who like to live in darkness and keep things shrouded in secret, turn on the lights, find the door, and get out. Don't let darkness become too comfortable for you, but expose it all to the light.

Confess—One of the best ways to turn on the light is to talk about your sin by confessing it to another person. When you confess, sin scampers off like cockroaches running from the light being turned on in a dark room. Don't be afraid to expose your sin. It might feel like it's killing you, but all it's killing is the cockroaches of darkness.

Pray It

Dear God, Please shine the light on all of my life. Don't let me live in darkness anymore. I want to be free from the stuff that I have hidden. I don't want to be controlled by sin any longer. Show me where I am living in the dark, and help me to live in your beautiful light. Amen.

Day 20

Goodness

Why Is It So Hard to Be Good?

Those who are in the flesh cannot please God.
Romans 8:8 ESV

If goodness came naturally to you, then it wouldn't be a fruit of the Spirit. So don't get down on yourself when you consider how bad you may be. You aren't alone; none of us are good by nature. That's because the flesh cannot please God; therefore the flesh is powerless to make you good (see Rom. 8:3, 8). But the flesh surrounds you. You live and breathe in it; you go to sleep in it and you wake up in it. You've listened to your flesh your entire life. You eat when it tells you it's hungry, and you cry when it tells you to cry. The flesh controls you all day long, so it's easy to respond to the flesh in order to please it and to keep it from melting down on you.

When you act on your flesh, you feel something and then you do it. The flesh responds to emotions and lets your emotions determine what is best for you. But the Holy Spirit often wants you to go against your flesh, and that's when the trouble hits. The flesh, grown so strong from years of being fed by your will, often overpowers the Spirit and shouts louder, and so it steals your attention. Then goodness flies out the window. The answer to this inability to subdue your flesh and to insist on the will of the Spirit lies in changing what's important to you. When your comfort, your hopes, your dreams, your life in this world are the focus of your day and the object of your desire, then it becomes second nature to respond to the flesh that wants the very same thing. But the Spirit wants something altogether different for your life. He wants God's glory over yours, and sometimes that means that the stuff you want is in direct opposition to his will. When what seems good to you is in conflict with what God says is good, your rebellion can take root.

But if you believe in the goodness of God and you believe that what he deems good is better for you than anything you want, then you can resist the urge to covet the stuff of this world. You can begin to turn yourself over to the voice of the Holy Spirit that guides you to the good things of God. It's a very simple equation, really. Do you believe that God is good? Can you accept that his goodness is the best thing for you? If you can, then why would you want anything that he didn't give you? Why would you choose to define goodness yourself, knowing full well that he is perfect and knows everything that you need?

If you want goodness in your life, you have to stop trying to define it and find it yourself, but instead accept God's definition of what is good—and not just what is good for him but what is good for you. You fail at being good because you don't really agree with God on what is good. You make up your own definition of goodness, and when his conflicts with yours, you choose yours. But true goodness becomes natural to you when you stop giving yourself permission to reject God's goodness. A lot of the failure you experience in the area of being good has to do with the fact that you make allowances for yourself to cheat and to avoid God's plans for your life, found in his Word. But when you determine that his Word has all that you need for life, then you search his Word for more knowledge and more insight on what is good to him so that it might be good to you too.

Define It

Just in case you forgot, in the "Define It" space below, write your definition of goodness based on what you've read so far. Then look up how I define goodness in the back of the book and write it in your own words under "Reword It."

Define It: Goodness

Reword It: Goodness

According to this definition, what would be the opposite of goodness? Can you think of some things in your life that are the opposite of goodness?

• **Ask It**

What do you covet that isn't yours?

How has your idea of "good" for you been different from God's?

God considers community a good thing. In Genesis he said it was not good for man to be alone (see Gen. 2:18), and all over the New Testament he talks about the importance of loving one another, encouraging one another, helping one another, and caring for one another. Do you believe that Christian community is good? Or have you given up Christian community for another kind of community?

God says that trusting him is good, and so living in fear is not good for you, because it is the opposite of trust. Consider your life and the things you fear. Can you agree with God that trust is good for you and so reject the fear in your life? What fears are you willing to say good-bye to today and reject the next time they try to drive you away from goodness?

• Pray It

Dear God, I want what you want for my life. Teach me what goodness is and give me the desire for more of it in my life. I confess that I have gone after the things that weren't good, but now I want only what you want. Thank you for showing me the fruit of the Spirit called goodness and giving me a desire for more of it. Amen.

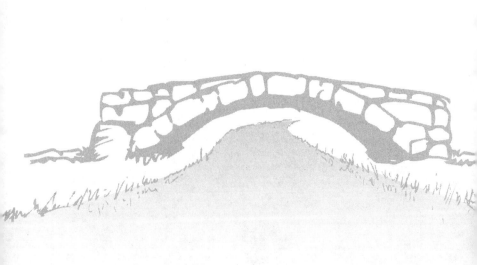

Day 21

Goodness

Finding Goodness

Try to discern what is pleasing to the Lord.
Ephesians 5:10

If goodness is anything that is pleasing to God, how do you make his pleasure the focus of your life? There are so many things that demand your time, so many things to think about and do—how do you find the energy or the strength to make goodness the goal of your life? The answer to that lies in your mind. Not that you already know it, but your mind *is* the answer, or, rather, your *renewed* mind is the answer. In Romans 12:2 Paul writes, "Do not be conformed to this world, but be transformed by *the renewal of your mind*, that by testing you may discern what is the will of God, what is good and acceptable and perfect" (emphasis added). It is through this renewal of your mind that you can know the goodness of God and his will. But how does this happen? How is your mind renewed?

Well, first of all, renewing your mind means getting rid of the old one. You do that by breaking your old way of thinking. It's been your pattern for a long time, so it's not going to be natural to change it, but the old way of thinking is grounded in the flesh. It started when you were born. As a baby you responded to the flesh. When it was hungry you cried, when it was happy you laughed, when it was tired you slept. Nothing drove your choices but your flesh. But as you grew and became aware of morals, you began to have a choice—a choice between self and others, a choice between good and bad, all of it based on pleasing your parents or the adults around you and how that affected your flesh. As you later became aware of God's Holy Spirit and your unlimited access to him, you began to hear not only your own thoughts but his as well. So your mind, being set on the things of the flesh since birth, had to be renewed, or changed, to adapt to the life of the Spirit. The things that are natural to your flesh, like looking out for yourself, pleasing yourself, judging others, gossiping, complaining, fearing, worrying—all of these old patterns of thought and emotion began to contradict the life of the Spirit in you. So this renewal began with your identification with Christ and your desire to be more like him.

As you begin to see who Christ is, you begin to see his character, and as you see that and read about it in his Word, you are seeing the new pattern that your mind is meant to take. At first this new pattern of thought and emotion might seem strange. As you read what pleases him and what doesn't, you start rejecting the things your flesh has come to expect, and this change in pattern pulls and tugs at you, making it difficult to adapt to. But over time, as you listen to the Holy Spirit on a daily basis and give your thoughts and life over to him, the change in pattern starts to become second nature. The more you read God's thoughts and see his pleasure, the more you want it, and the more your old mind gets renewed. Then those things that used to be so natural to your flesh change, but soon you see other things that were buried so deep that you never saw them. Those need renewal as well. In turning your life over to the Holy Spirit to search and to expose the areas of sin in your life, you unearth all kinds of stuff that is part of the old you, and you give it up. As you do this, your mind is renewed and the old way of living becomes less and less natural and the fruit of the Spirit more and more natural.

If you want more goodness in your life, then you must begin by renewing your mind. Find out what pleases God and what pleases you, see how those differ, and then choose his way, because in his pleasure is all of your goodness and joy.

Renew It

What are three areas in your life that need to be renewed? Do you struggle with fear, worry, bitterness, hate, or anger? Think about those areas in your life where you are living with an old mind, one set on the things of the flesh.

The renewed mind looks at the things that used to plague the old mind differently. What are some ways that you might look at those things differently? If you don't know, then pray and ask God. Spend time in the Bible looking up what he has to say about these particular things.

When your mind is renewed, your mouth is too. Do you speak with goodness? Think about the words you use, including the kinds of words and the amount of words. In what ways might that change when you have a renewed mind?

Matthew 12:35 says, "The good person out of his good treasure brings forth good, and the evil person out of his evil treasure brings forth evil." Write down all of the things you treasure in your life.

Now, are those things you treasure good in God's eyes? Consider each one and how what you treasure may or may not distract you or pull you away from God. How might you change what you treasure? By giving up those treasures that war against your devotion to God. Pray today to give up those bad treasures to God and to replace them with his Holy Spirit as your treasure.

Pray It

Dear God, I want to live with a renewed mind. I don't want to think the way I used to think. I don't want to respond to my flesh but to your Spirit. Please teach me to love what you love and to want what you want so that my flesh is rejected. Amen.

Day 22

Faithfulness

Faithfulness Does What Is True

Finally, brothers and sisters, whatever is true, whatever is noble, whatever is right, whatever is pure, whatever is lovely, whatever is admirable—if anything is excellent or praiseworthy—think about such things.

Philippians 4:8 NIV

God is faithful. If he were not faithful, that would mean he was a liar and as such could not be trusted. But by his very nature he is always faithful, and he wants the same thing for his kids. In fact, the family of faith depends on it. After all, how can we have Christian community if we aren't faithful and no one can be trusted? **Faithfulness agrees with God that whatever is true is essential in the life of faith.**

Faithfulness does what is true, noble, right, pure, lovely, and admirable. Not what seems the best or makes the most sense, but what is true. That's why Paul encourages us to think about such things: because where your thoughts are, so is your heart and your mind.

Faithfulness is never deceptive. It doesn't cheat or lie; it doesn't hide in the dark and disguise itself. Faithfulness is honest, even about sin. That doesn't mean being proud of your sin when you are faithful but means that you aren't afraid to confess it and even to talk about sins that you no longer struggle with. Allowing the saving work of Christ on the sin in your life to be an example and encouragement to others is a part of faithfulness. Hiding is not.

Faithfulness starts in relationship to God. Without faith there can be no true faithfulness, because as a fruit of the Spirit, your faithfulness is a gift of the Spirit, not of works, so you can't boast about how faithful you are. No, faithfulness is a gift from God.

Like all other fruit, faithfulness doesn't just benefit those around you; it also has some benefits for you personally. They come in the area of protecting you from self-deception. Self-deception is one of the most insidious forms of unfaithfulness because you are lying to yourself, and when you do that you are standing on a false foundation. Self-deception comes when you pervert God's law and make it something that it isn't, like the perfectionist who makes it a law that she has to be perfect in everything she does, or the anorexic who makes it a law to be thin. When you create any law in your life other than God's, you are being unfaithful in your self-deception. That is a recipe for disaster, because living under self-imposed law makes you a slave to that law, and that makes you a slave to sin, which leads to death (see Rom. 6:16). So self-deception is self-destruction. But faithfulness to God and his Word is life.

Faithfulness has to do with honesty between you and God, as well as you and yourself. But it also has to do with doing what you say and saying what you mean. It doesn't mean being brutally honest, because that would be inconsistent with the fruit of kindness, but it does mean loving others enough to be real, transparent, and kind all at once. If you want more faithfulness in your life, now is the time to step forward and receive it. The Holy Spirit is waiting to give you more of it in your life—it's there for the asking.

Faithfulness is a part of the nature of a God Girl because she is a child of God who himself is ever faithful. So faithfulness isn't just about being true to those you love, defending them against others, or never leaving them, but it's about living in the truth of God's Word. It's not about being faithful to other people so much as it is about being faithful to God.

Check It

Think about your faithfulness. Are you faithful to people because you love them, or because God's Word asks you to be faithful? What is your faithfulness based on?

Is there anything that would keep you from being faithful? Like another person's unfaithfulness, sin, etc.?

Does God put conditions on faithfulness?

How can you be faithful when someone has been unfaithful to you?

Are there relationships where you have been unfaithful to God? If so, confess your sin to God, who took the brunt of your unfaithfulness, and repent. Turn away from your sin and vow to stay faithful to him and so to those around you.

● Pray It

> *Dear God, teach me to be faithful to you. Help me to see that faithfulness is grounded in who you are, not who those around me are. Let me see your faithfulness and imitate it in my own life. Amen.*

Day 23

Faithfulness

Faithfulness Doesn't Overreact

*But whoever does what is true comes to the light, so that
it may be clearly seen that his works have been carried out
in God.*

John 3:21

*The heart of man plans his way, but the LORD establishes
his steps.*

Proverbs 16:9

*L*ight has a way of making things clear. It exposes the
stuff that used to hide in darkness and gives you the
ability to see what needs to be cleaned up. As a God
Girl you are meant to live in the light, to expose the darkness, and to be always faithful. **The faithful girl who lives
in the light doesn't overreact to the world around her or**

within her. Overreacting has to do with making something more important than it is. For a lot of girls, this is a normal response brought on by the depth of emotion they feel. They act in response to their feelings, rather than responding to the Spirit. This produces unfaithfulness.

When what you feel trumps what God says, then you become a drama queen, giving in to all the situations that are meant to test and shape you, not to destroy you. Over-reaction is seeing the world through doubt-colored glasses. This kind of doubt comes from believing that the situation is bigger than God can handle. Since it's so big, it must mean he has left the building, he's gone off and left you, and there is no hope. A lot of times this happens when you make a mistake. When you want to please God, when you want to succeed, when you want to be loved and you fail, it's easy to think either that your mess is impossible for God to fix or that you deserve punishment for messing things up. This attitude assumes that you or anyone else can change God's plan and do something totally out of his ability to manage. When that's your idea of God, then the worry and fear over what has happened can overwhelm you. But the truth is that nothing can thwart God's plans.

So your faithfulness relies on your idea of God's faithfulness. If you doubt he can do what he says he can do, like work all things together for the good of those who love him (see Rom. 8:28) or establish your steps (see Prov. 16:9), then you are going to freak out when things look bleak. But all of your freaking out just tells your heart and anyone who is watching that you don't think God is God enough to manage your problem. Your faithfulness rests on his faithfulness. If you don't trust him, then you cannot be faithful, because your doubt leads you to faithlessness.

Faithfulness doesn't overreact to anything that happens, because overreacting makes you unreliable as a witness and as a tool in the hands of God. You cannot be unreliable and faithful at the same time. This goes for more than drama; it also has to do with your words not being true. Faithfulness has to do with trustworthiness. If you say one thing and do another, then you are not letting the fruit of faithfulness grow in your life. The inconsistent life is contradictory to faithfulness. So any kind of double life, any kind of hypocrisy— pretending to be something you are not in order to impress or deceive—is an insidious fruit of the flesh that will lead to your destruction as it battles against the life of the Spirit and pulls you farther and farther away from God.

Pretending to be something you are not by hiding your sin in the dark, all in order to protect yourself, is actually an act of self-deception. You are deceiving yourself into believing that playing pretend has any kind of reward at all. All it does is harden your heart to the only One who can save you. In your faithfulness don't let the things that happen around you control you, make you doubt the sovereignty of God, or lead you to take matters into your own hands.

Think about It

What does it mean to be true?

Are you prone to overreacting? If so, what is your idea of who God is when it comes to your circumstances? Do you consider him faithful?

Exaggeration is another form of unfaithfulness. Think about your words. How many times do you exaggerate things? Why do you believe you have to stretch the truth? What is the goal of exaggeration?

Think about your life. Do you have two lives? Are you a different person with different people? Why do you feel the need to pose? What is at the root of it?

Are there any relationships where you have been unreliable? In what ways, and how can you change your pattern?

● **Pray It**

Dear God, please show me your faithfulness when things get out of hand. Help me to remember that you are always in control no matter how much it looks like you aren't. Amen.

• Light It

Today, turn the lights on your speech. In every situation, pay attention to your desire to overreact or exaggerate. Every time you do, remember God's faithfulness and his desire for you to imitate him. Try to use fewer words so that you can have more time to think about him, to correct your course, and to respond in faith. Too many words makes it easy to lose control. Slow down today and find faithfulness.

Day 24

Faithfulness

Finding Faithfulness

Let not steadfast love and faithfulness forsake you; bind them around your neck; write them on the tablet of your heart.

Proverbs 3:3

*F*aithfulness as a concept can be hard to explain. Most might think it means you are loyal and devoted to a person. And as long as that person is God, then that definition is right, but as soon as your loyalty rests on another human being rather than God, it is no longer a fruit of the Spirit. The fruit of the Spirit called faithfulness is generated by the Holy Spirit, not by your love or devotion to a human being. Your faithfulness to others should be an outpouring of your faithfulness to him, and that's why you can be faithful to friends, strangers, and enemies alike. What this means is that you are a God Girl no matter who you are with. You are faithful no matter how faithless others are. In other words, the faithlessness, cruelty, or hate of the world never changes who you are, never leads you to compromise or to choose sin. When the faithfulness of God defines you, you are a safe person for everyone because you point everyone to Christ, regardless of their faithfulness in return.

Faithfulness means that you are not overly defensive, treating others as the enemy, but that you treat others as either fellow disciples of Christ, members of your family of faith, or as nonbelievers you are meant to be a witness to. Because your life points up to the life of Christ rather than inward to the life of self, you find no need to be self-defensive. He is all that matters. Because of that you will not be prone to jealousy. Jealousy comes from a faithless life. It points to a distrust of God and accuses him of being unkind, unfair, and partial to others, when you know his love for you is pure and true. Faithfulness ignores the pangs of envy and keeps faith in God.

When you allow the Holy Spirit to give you faithfulness, that faithfulness is a guide to others around you, not a stumbling block. That means that when you see sin in your friend's life, you refuse to encourage it by covering for them, sympathizing with them, or joining them. Faithfulness doesn't forsake God's will in order to protect a friend. That is the definition of unfaithfulness: turning away from the Holy Spirit in order to encourage someone else's sin. So the God Girl speaks truth and encourages her friend to forsake her sin and to listen to God's Word and the voice of the Holy Spirit. This is faithfulness to both God and friend.

When you are faithful, you want only what's best, even if what's best for another might be worse for you. A lot of times the failures or weaknesses of others can become the subject of conversation so that others can pray for them or just to bond with another person over the mess of someone else's life. But faithfulness doesn't allow you to talk about someone else, even under the guise of wanting to pray for them. Faithfulness is so fully focused on God and his will that any discussion of another person's sin is irrelevant, unless that person has asked for you to tell others. The idea that it's okay to talk about other people in order to feel like you are in the know, are better than they are, or are "looking out for them" is a lie. Talking about other people is unfaithful because it draws on the flesh that desires what Adam and Eve desired in the Garden: to have all the knowledge in the world. Faithfulness leaves omniscience to God and trusts him with the lives of others.

Faithfulness comes not from your love for others but from your love for God and his faithfulness. Don't let your unfaithfulness make the claim that God can't be trusted, but react to everyone in your life with the same faithfulness God has given you.

Explore It

Enemies—Do you have any? If there is a person you resent or want to hurt, then you have an enemy. Considering the idea of faithfulness, what do you think God wants you to do in regard to this person? Pray for them today and ask God how you are to treat them next time you see them.

Frenemies—If you have a friend who is sometimes an enemy, then you have someone who may be leading you to sin. It may be because you want to get even with them or because they're leading you to some other kind of sin. Think about the people in your life who encourage your sin, either by their actions against you or by their encouragement of your sinning with them. A frenemy is a difficult relationship, but God's faithfulness still has to define all your relationships. What does God want you to do with regard to this person? Pray for them, resist them, disengage from them, or speak with them in love? Ask God today what to do when your friend turns on you.

Taking sides—Are there any relationships you are in now where you find yourself taking sides? Our God is a God of reconciliation, not separation. Pray for these relationships today and ask God how you can be more faithful in them.

• Pray It

Dear God, teach me to know what is faithful and what isn't. Help me to be a good friend and a loving enemy. Give me guidance in relationship to difficult people, and help me to serve you no matter what might happen. Amen.

• Hold It

Today, if you have an opportunity to criticize someone, hold your tongue. Instead, pray for them and yourself. Ask God to show you how you can help them rather than judge them. Remain faithful to him, and stay out of the battles of life. Instead, be an interceder, asking for God's will to be done in the lives of those around you.

Day 25

Gentleness

Gentleness Trusts God

A person cannot receive even one thing unless it is given him from heaven.

John 3:27

As a God Girl you have access to a life of tranquility, of calm, and of rest. Your spirit doesn't have to be on edge or stressed out. But when the Holy Spirit animates your life, there is a carefreeness to you that others only wish they could experience. The fruit of the Spirit called gentleness, also known as meekness, gives an easiness to life, even in the middle of turmoil and suffering. When the world around you explodes into uncertainty or anger, the Spirit speaks serenity to your soul, and because of that you don't need to accuse God of anything by complaining or scratching your way out of your pit.

See, the God Girl knows that God has it all under control. No, not just that, but he is *behind* it all, not just managing it but allowing it in order that all of it might serve his holy and beautiful purpose. When you have the Holy Spirit living inside of you, his presence assures you that God can be trusted no matter how dark life gets. To the world without the Spirit, this sense of calm and tranquility might look like insanity; after all, things need to be worried about, stressed over, and managed. You can't just be calm and trust in an unseen God who is letting everything fall down around you. That's just craziness! To the world without hope in a loving and kind God, that seems true—things must be done to fix things. But the God Girl isn't like the world. And so her spirit isn't like theirs, all chaotic and stressed out.

In fact, when she enters the room, her gentleness comes with her, no matter what the mood around her. How many times have you let the spirit of the room change you? Have you ever gotten into a situation that has totally ruined your mood, brought you down, or bummed you out? When that happens it's because you are no longer being informed by the Holy Spirit but are controlled by the spirit of the situation. Whether it's anger, fear, hatred, or stress, when it screams at you and you allow it to pull you into doubting the hand of God, gentleness fades away and frustration, bitterness, sarcasm, harshness, resentment, and a whole bunch of other yucky emotions take its place.

Why do you feel so stressed out by life? Because you haven't understood that the Holy Spirit has been offering you gentleness, and not so that you can be steamrolled by life, a wallflower who nobody bothers to notice, but so that you can show others that life doesn't have to be bitter or harsh and that you don't have to be thrown around by it like a boat tossed about on a rough sea. Gentleness is evidence of the life of Christ in you. It is his fingerprint on your life; it is his spiritual DNA running through you. It is the power of the blood that left his body and now covers your soul.

As a God Girl your life is meant to be different; it is meant to be gentle. And it can be, not because you are lying to yourself about the world around you but because you know that "a person cannot receive even one thing unless it is given him from heaven" (John 3:27). And that means that all of it—the good, the bad, and the ugly—is all from the Perfect One, and therefore it is all perfect. So why stress about the gifts of God, whether they are what you had hoped for or not? After all, is there anything in this whole world that you would want if you knew that God didn't think it was the best thing for you?

• Define It

Okay, it's time to "Define It." What can you say about gentleness from what you've read so far?

Define It: Gentleness

Now go to the Dictionary in the back of this book to see how I define it. Then rewrite that def in your own words.

Reword It: Gentleness

● **Find It**

What do you want that God hasn't given you? Or that he has taken from you?

Take a look at Matthew 26:38–39. Can you tell God, "Not my will but yours be done"? Why or why not?

What areas in your life make you feel out of control?

How might the fruit of the Spirit called gentleness affect those feelings?

A gentle spirit doesn't accuse God, fight with him, or complain about the things he has allowed. Have you accused God by complaining about the stuff in your life?

Look up Philippians 2:14 and write it here:

Why do you think God tells us not to complain?

What does your complaint say about God?

What kinds of things do you complain about the most?

• Pray It

> *Dear God, I confess my pride. I have not been gentle but have been harsh and whiny. I have accused you of not being a good Father by my complaint, worry, and stress. I haven't let you grow the fruit of gentleness in my life, but I am ready to reject my flesh and to listen to your Spirit. Teach me gentleness. Grow it in my life and help me to trust you even when things look bad. I want more of you in my life. I want the fruit of gentleness. I want to be more like Christ. Thank you for hearing my prayer and for showing me the areas in my life where I have missed out on listening to your gentle voice. I love you. Amen.*

• Don't Complain

Today, refuse to complain about anything. When you feel a complaint coming on, zip it! Remind yourself that what you are about to complain about went through God for approval, and he deemed it good for you. So don't accuse him of being evil or unkind; it isn't in his nature to be either.

Be encouraging. Smile. Look on the bright side. Look for the good in every situation, and share your gentleness with others.

Find hope and something to be thankful for. Every time you want to voice a complaint, stop and turn it around. Find something you can compliment, appreciate, or at least thank God for. It's too hot today? Thank God for the sun that keeps our earth warm and lit. Are you exhausted? Thank God for nighttime and the gift of sleep.

Day 26

Gentleness

The Opposite of Gentleness Is Pride

Whoever exalts himself will be humbled, and whoever humbles himself will be exalted.

Matthew 23:12 ESV

In order to understand gentleness, it is important to understand pride. If gentleness has to do with humility and meekness, then the opposite of gentleness is pride, and it's the foundation of all your troubles, the beginning of all of your sin. It is pride that says, "I deserve more than this," that covets what others have, that is jealous, vengeful, angry, resentful, bitter, depressed, combative, lustful, hopeless, and the list goes on and on. Any sin can be listed along with these, because **sin is the flesh's attempt to accuse God, to contradict him, or to get out from under his**

control. Its fuel is the self-adoration or worship of self that tells you that you are worth more than what you've got. This selfishness that is a part of the nature of all of us since the fall of Adam and Eve compels us to sin in order to get what we want. So all of the sin that you struggle with has its root in pride.

As a fruit of the flesh, pride grows as you set your mind on the things of the flesh. As we saw in Romans 8:6–8, "For to set the mind on the flesh is death, but to set the mind on the Spirit is life and peace. For the mind that is set on the flesh is hostile to God, for it does not submit to God's law; indeed, it cannot. Those who are in the flesh cannot please God" (ESV). So the mind set on the flesh produces the opposite of gentleness and wreaks havoc on your life. In pride you lash out when others criticize you. **In pride you know that your ways are better than theirs, and so you try to control or manipulate them.** In pride you refuse to submit to those in authority over you because you are sure you know better. And **in pride you believe that you should be perfect,** and if you aren't, then you become angry or depressed, worried or self-loathing. **Pride is at the root of all your sin, all of it.** Even the stuff that looks like low self-esteem is really pride, because it says, "I am so lowly, so uniquely a failure, not even God can love me. I'm just that special." But this prideful way of thinking is a fruit of the flesh and a destructive growth in your life. As your life gets set on the things of this world, God gets pushed aside, and with him the nutrients and power needed to grow the fruit of the Spirit.

But it doesn't have to stay that way. You can reject the fruit of the flesh in favor of the fruit of the Spirit, and all it takes is a mindfulness of what God has done and is doing in your life. Once your spiritual eyes are opened to the fruit, once you see that the opposite of gentleness is pride and you see how pride shows up in your life, you can start to reject it. You can't get rid of a problem you know nothing about. Blissful ignorance of sin is the best way to grow more sin. But once you are aware of the sin in your life, it's easier to get rid of it and to turn instead to the things of the Spirit. The Holy Spirit is here, and he is waiting to speak truth to you and grow the fruit of gentleness in your life. Now that you are both on the same page, progress will be astronomically faster. Knowledge is power. The truth will set you free, not just from ignorance but from the pain of ignorance and the pride that keeps you from gentleness. Set your mind on the truth today. Turn to God's Word and discover his gentle nature, look to him over self, reject the parts of you that are inconsistent with the life of Christ in you, and allow the fruit of the Spirit room to grow in your life.

Define It

Define It: Pride

Reword It: Pride

What are some synonyms for pride?

• Verse It

Matthew 23:12

Proverbs 11:2

James 4:6

• Find It

Are there some areas in your life that you struggle to control? Can you see pride at the root of them?

What is the value of self-esteem?

What is the danger of self-esteem?

Take a look at this verse again: "Whoever exalts himself will be humbled, and whoever humbles himself will be exalted" (Matt. 23:12).

What happens to the prideful in this verse?

What happens to the humble?

● **Pray It**

Dear God, today show me how to be gentle and meek. Kill my pride and reveal to me the areas in my life where I am acting on pride. Give me ears to hear you today, Lord. Amen.

● **Be Teachable**

Today, allow others to correct you, to criticize you, or to reject you. As they do, consider that it isn't just them but may be God who is also speaking to you, wanting to show you something in your life that is destroying you. Ask him what he wants to show you through their words or actions. Ask him not to change them but to change you. When you allow it to be about changing you rather than others, you find the fruit of gentleness growing, and with that comes the serenity and calmness of a life spent completely for him.

When someone corrects you, refuse to defend yourself or to argue. Thank them and tell them you will work on it and that you are sorry to have offended or hurt them. Allow this moment to humiliate you, thus teaching your heart humility. Don't fear rejection or worry about what people think, but set your mind on pleasing God.

Carry this verse with you today: "For am I now seeking the approval of man, or of God? Or am I trying to please man? If I were still trying to please man, I would not be a servant of Christ" (Gal. 1:10 ESV). Memorize it. Record it, make a song out of it, do what you can to make it your verse. And remember who you live to please. When he becomes your sole focus, you will become emotionally and spiritually bulletproof. Though the pains of life may fly at you like a bullet set on killing you, because you are bulletproof, they will not succeed. Sure, you may be knocked to the ground, but your skin will not be pierced and your heart will not stop.

Day 27

Gentleness

Gentleness Is Selfless

Let your gentleness be evident to all. The Lord is near.
Philippians 4:5 NIV

*G*entleness changes the way you see and interact with others. It all comes from the fact that gentleness, seen in your humility, is about who God is, not who you are. In order to put God in the girl, the girl must first acknowledge her need for him. She must see her complete inability not only to save herself but to serve herself, to help herself, or to control herself. She must acknowledge her absolute dependence on him. This is what happens at the point of salvation: complete and utter humility in accepting that you can't do it on your own. In this moment, you **admit to God that this world isn't yours but that it is his, and that you can't manage it or change it as you had hoped you could.**

This is the essence of gentleness. In this humble state, you are then able to look at the rest of the world and see not a bunch of terrible losers, cruel abusers, or angry users, but broken and weak human beings who, like you, can't save themselves and are trapped in the same quagmire of sin as you are. "For all have sinned and fallen short of the glory of God" (Rom. 3:23 ESV). When you realize that others are no worse than you but are equally sinful and evil in heart, then you can find the strength to be gentle with them, even when they are harsh with you.

The fruit of the Spirit called gentleness feeds those around you with an unexpected delight, because gentleness gets you outside of yourself. When that happens you are no longer focused on the pain and suffering in your life, and so you are less consumed with the trials of life. As you become less consumed with that stuff, you are less likely to over-react and you become less combative, bitter, and belligerent. This makes you easy to be around, even when you make a mistake. Even when you stumble and fail to be the God Girl you are meant to be, it's okay, because you don't add insult to injury by getting mad because someone calls you on your sin or because they react in a negative way to your actions or words. When you allow the Holy Spirit to produce the fruit of gentleness in your life instead of going with your flesh, you are interested in him, not yourself. And a girl who is interested in him over herself takes everything in stride. She gladly accepts correction, easily confesses her mistakes, and quickly listens when others admonish or even accuse her.

See, it is the nature of your self to protect itself, to fight for your rights, to argue with dissenters of those "rights." Because of this pride, your self gets you into all kinds of battles with the other human beings around you. **When you feed them the fruit of gentleness, you aren't looking out for yourself at all, but you are looking to serve the God you love and**

146

to feed his sheep. How can you feed them the rotten fruit of pride when he has been so gentle with you? How can you reject the trying situations he allows in your life and instead fight or push against them as if they weren't meant for you and must be rejected, as if you deserve more? Gentleness knows better. Gentleness compels a teachable spirit, one that wants what God wants over all else and so is willing to be corrected if it means that it will help you to reject another attempt of your pride to drive you to partner with your flesh rather than your God.

Gentleness softens your heart and your words. It keeps you from argument, self-defensiveness, and pride because it trusts God even with mean people. Rather than fight back, it bows down and asks God what this attack is meant to prune in the life of faith. Cutting the gnarled and broken branches from the vine isn't pleasant and peaceful, but it must happen in order for the vine to produce much fruit. So it is in the life of the girl who wants to grow abundant fruit for the kingdom—she must accept the pruning that comes even at the hands of others, knowing full well that God uses other humans to cut and clean his precious branches so that they may flourish and live an abundant life.

Think about It

What are some synonyms for gentleness?

What's the opposite of gentleness?

• Verse It

Matthew 5:5

Colossians 3:12

James 3:13

• Find It

In what relationships in your life do you find it hard to be gentle?

Why?

What things do you think when one of these people pushes your buttons?

What are some antonyms to "gentleness" that describe how you react to the button-pushers in your life?

What are you thinking when you react this way? Consider your thoughts and what you think about the people you find difficult to deal with.

Look at this list and think about how these things might be fruit of the flesh, pride, rather than fruit of the Spirit, gentleness. Do any of these describe you?

Being harsh with people

Arguing

Trying to control others

Being a busybody

Impoliteness

Being unteachable

Wanting vengeance

Perfectionism

Being loud or showy

Wanting to be the center of attention

How might the Spirit of gentleness change these things in your life?

• Pray It

Dear God, show me my pride today. Teach me how pride is at the root of all of my trouble. I no longer want to think of myself first or even second. I want to think of you first and others second. Help me to get over myself and to trust you and to love others. Give me the fruit of gentleness today. Amen.

• Be Polite

Politeness might not seem like a spiritual value, but it is a behavior that comes with a life of gentleness. Politeness says that others matter and that you want them to know. It can be as simple as saying thank you every time somebody does something nice, even if it's something they do every day. Being polite carries a lot of the aroma of God with it because politeness cares for others the way God cares for you. No matter how small the ways, will you be polite today? Will you say please and thank you, even if someone is just doing their job? Be polite to those who are impolite, mean, or angry. Don't let their sin be an excuse for yours.

Day 28

Self-Control

Self-Control Denies Self

If anyone would come after me, let him deny himself and take up his cross and follow me.

Mark 8:34

Self-control is a fruit of the Spirit. It isn't the source of all the other fruit, but it does impact how the Holy Spirit operates in your life. Because the word *self* figures so prominently in the word *self-control*, it's easy to apply self-help ideas to getting yourself more under control. It can be easy to think it's about working hard at mastering something you really want in or out of your life. But that's a wrong approach to the life of self-control. It's more about turning yourself over to someone than controlling yourself. In other words, self-control has to do with subduing your self and surrendering it to God. It has to do with stopping your

151

self-life from reigning supreme and instead putting it under the authority of the Holy Spirit. In this way you don't control through the power of self, but your self is controlled by the Holy Spirit, to whom you have surrendered all authority.

When you think about all of the areas where you lack the fruit of the Spirit, it can be easy to freak out and think you have so much work to do. But that's not true. **What really needs to take place is surrender**. It goes like this. Each time that you are tempted to sin and to obey your flesh, you simply turn your thoughts and actions over to the Holy Spirit and rely on him to direct your ways. Each time you do this, sin will become less and less automatic, and the fruit will become more and more abundant. That's because it isn't by your power that any of this fruit grows, but it's by his and his alone. But in order for that to happen, you have to give up; you have to stop trying to do it by your own strength and instead relinquish control to the Holy Spirit.

When you see areas in your life where you lack fruit, **self-control involves giving up the effort and instead turning your mind toward God's thoughts on the subject**. As you start to read in his Word about the fruit and to learn his thoughts and make them a part of your life, his Holy Spirit will make the fruit a part of your life as well. So it isn't this tough job you have to do to control yourself, but it's a commitment you have to make in order to make his thoughts more important than yours. See, **self-control isn't the act of turning your life over to your self to control; it isn't about believing in yourself, trusting yourself, or even loving yourself more, but it's about giving up your self to the life of the Holy Spirit.**

This might seem like a dangerous prospect, and that has kept many people from a life of surrender. But the truth is, to deny yourself and to take up your cross and follow Christ is to put your self-life to death in favor of the Holy Spirit. This self-death might sound dangerous—after all, who will care for you if you don't? But the truth is that it isn't until you die to self that you can live for Christ. You cannot live for both of you; if you try, you will end up putting yourself first more often than not. But the life of faith and abundant fruit is found in making him your obsession rather than yourself.

So **self-control has to do with giving up self rather than mastering it.** That's good news, because it means it isn't up to you beyond the point of surrender. Giving yourself up to him is your part. Then as you keep your mind on him as your Savior, rather than looking to self, you find yourself in possession of more self-control than you could ever dream of. Your self-control becomes his job once you give your self-life up to him.

Control It

In what areas of your life do you lack self-control?

How have you tried and failed to control yourself?

When you think about the idea of surrender, how do you feel? Does it scare you? Can you accept it? If not, what is your other option?

How would you define self-control based on what you've learned?

Do you want more self-control in your life? Spend some time with God now and surrender your life to the Holy Spirit.

What does it mean to die to self?

Are there areas in your life that are inconsistent with the life of Christ and need to die? How will you forsake them?

How does humility figure in with this death to self?

What does dying to self do to your pride?

- **Verse It**

    Matthew 10:38–39

    Matthew 20:16

    Luke 14:27

- **Try It**

    What areas in your life could use your death to self? To get you thinking, here are some areas where death is essential:

    Self-protection—involving fear, control, revenge, fights, bossiness

    Self-hate—involving guilt, self-injury, self-loathing

    Self-obsession—involving worry over looks, weight, future, grades, success, failure, pride

    Self-pleasure—involving comfort, lust, laziness, entertainment, perfectionism, obsessive-compulsiveness

    As you identify the areas in your life where there needs to be less of you in order for there to be more of him, confess your sin to God and promise repentance. Don't let your self-life become your God, but instead turn your life over to him and be free.

• Pray It

Dear God, I surrender all. I give up my life to you. I have tried to control myself and I cannot, but I trust you to give me self-control as a fruit of your Spirit. Please teach me your ways and give me your strength that I might not sin but instead choose to deny myself and take up my cross and follow you. Amen.

Day 29

Self-Control

Controlling Yourself

What is impossible with man is possible with God.
Luke 18:27

Self-control without God is completely impossible. It is ultimately impossible for humans to maintain self-control, and that's why we make so many resolutions to stop this or start that, and we fail time and time again. When what you resolve is to control yourself rather than to turn yourself over to the Holy Spirit, then your resolve will soon falter. So how do you do it? How do you surrender your life to the life of the Holy Spirit? Well, the first step is admitting that you have a problem. If you don't see any need in your life, if there is no sin that controls you, no area in your life where you can't control yourself, then why would you need him? This is why we can thank God for our weakness, because it is in our weakness that we are able to come to him and turn ourselves over to him. As Jesus said, the healthy person doesn't need a doctor (see Luke 5:31), and so Jesus came to seek and save the lost, not the ones who have it all covered themselves. **You must admit that you have a problem and that you need God in order to overcome it.** This is the act of confession—agreeing with God that you are a sinner in need of salvation.

Then you have to admit not only that you have a problem but also that you can't do anything about it. You are powerless to control yourself without him. You make commitments, but you keep messing up and giving in to sin. So you have to realize and then admit that you can't, you just can't—but that he can. After all, "what is impossible with man is possible with God" (Luke 18:27). Thank God for that! Then as you admit you can't do it, you surrender it to him and say, "You can." If you don't think God can manage your life—if you don't think he has the power to give you abundant fruit, faith, hope, and all that you need to live life here on earth—then you cannot go any further in faith. You must believe that he can. And a part of believing that he can is adoring the fact that he can. In other words, when you see his majesty and power, you can't help but talk about it, worship it, proclaim it. So a part of self-control is adoration, reminding yourself that he is able. If you cannot adore God, then you must find out more about him, because once you know who he is, you can't help but adore him, and as you do, you stop worshiping yourself because you see that you are not him. This is the beautiful part of surrender: it allows you to fully adore him and to give up trying to prove yourself or hold yourself in a higher regard than you should.

In order to turn your life over to God, you must give up trying to be your own little god, and that means you have to reject the laws you have created for yourself in order to try to make yourself good enough. Beyond that, you have to take a look at how much of *God's* law you have dismissed as unimportant or unnecessary for your salvation. It is true that obedience doesn't save you—only his death and resurrection can do that—but when you accept disobedience in your life for the "little" sins, it only feeds your lack of self-control. When you decide that it's okay to break the law as long as you don't get caught, what you are really doing is training yourself in self-rule rather than self-control. And when you say that your lack of self-control is an acceptable sin, then you lose control not just in one area of your life but in all as you turn yourself away from the Holy Spirit and toward self. Your lack of self-control should bother you, not confirm you are only human. If you want to gain more self-control, consider controlling your passions even in areas that aren't necessarily sinful by turning your whole life over to him. Allow his thoughts to be the fuel for your action.

Admit It

Looking at the areas where you lack self-control allows you to spot the places where you have surrendered your life to stuff rather than to God. Look at your lack of self-control, your obsessions, and your passions to see if any of them point to you living your life for yourself rather than for Christ. Ask God what he would have you do in these areas in order to die to self and to live more fully for him.

How much time do you spend thinking about God, praying, studying, and concentrating on his Word? Are there things in your life you can give up in order to find more time for thoughts about God? If you can give up thirty minutes of time spent on things that aren't God so that you can spend thirty minutes with God, then add that thirty minutes to your morning and devote your life to him before you are tempted to devote it to anything else tomorrow and the next day.

Pray It

God has provided spiritual protection for your mind and heart and emotions. It's called the armor of God, and while it might seem like just a nice idea, it is more than that. It is actual protection for your mind and for the benefit of the fruit of self-control in your life. If you don't know how to put it on, then just pray these words to God, based on Ephesians 6:13–18, and put the armor on your life each day:

> *God, today I take up the whole armor of God, that I may be able to withstand in the evil day, and having done all, to stand firm. I will stand, therefore, having fastened on the belt of truth, and having put on the breastplate of righteousness, and as shoes for my feet having put on the readiness given by the gospel of peace. In all circumstances I will take up the shield of faith, with which I can extinguish all the flaming darts of the evil one, and the helmet of salvation, and the sword of the Spirit, which is the Word of God, praying at all times in the Spirit. To that end I will keep alert with all perseverance, making supplication for all the saints. Amen.*

Day 30

Self-Control

Wrapping Up the Fruit

Like a city whose walls are broken through is a person who lacks self-control.

Proverbs 25:28 NIV

f you lack the fruit of the Spirit in your life, it is because you have trusted yourself too much. I know, you think that you don't trust yourself enough, that you doubt yourself and you think you are unworthy. All of these sayings might be stuff you say to yourself, but the lack of fruit in anyone's life comes from having too much confidence, not too little. That's why developing the fruit isn't about having more self-confidence, self-esteem, or self-control that gives you the strength and the power to grow and to be more. Any belief that you have the power to control yourself or to grow the fruit of the Spirit in your life is misguided and harmful to the life of faith.

If there is anything you learn from this study, any hope that you have, let it be that you can't do it, but God can, and he will as soon as you get out of the way and surrender your life over to him. **As long as you believe that it is impossible for you to have all this fruit of joy, peace, patience, self-control, and so on in your life because you've tried and failed, you will continue to fail.** Believing that God cannot do what God says he will do is a recipe for disaster. But his Word makes it clear that all of these things we have been talking about are the product of his presence in your life. Not only that, but they are meant for all believers, not just the few perfect ones. Yep, the fruit, all of it, is meant to be a part of your life, and because of that, when you stop relying on the self part of you that disagrees with God and instead insist that he can be trusted, the fruit will pour out of your life. It's the nature of the Holy Spirit to fill you abundantly with all of these things.

Unfortunately, **what happens for most of us in the area of fruitlessness is that we give ourselves permission to sin**. We don't verbalize it, but as we sin in little ways, we say, "I've just got to do this, or have this, or be this." Part of that speaks to the fact that you know that God isn't going to strike you down. Because of his grace you know that you have forgiveness, but giving yourself silent permission to fail is the quickest way to fail. Why do you lack self-control in some areas and not others? Because in those areas where you lack it, you have decided that it's okay to lose control. For example, you might think it's okay to lose control and gossip just a little. After all, who does it hurt? And you really, really have to get it out and tell someone. But this permission you give yourself wears away at your self-control in all areas. Like the kids' game of Don't Break the Ice that you might have played when you were little, each permission you give yourself to respond to your flesh rather than the

Spirit knocks an ice block of self-control out from under your whole life, weakening it in bigger and more important areas of your life.

If you want to grow more of the fruit of the Spirit in your life, then turn your mind and heart away from yourself and onto him. Reject the stuff that used to be natural to you, renew your mind, and surrender yourself to his Spirit. As you take time to study his Word, to learn more about the fruit, you will begin to find it becoming a supernatural part of your life. Then you will find yourself with a faith that is overflowing with more fruit than you could possibly imagine.

Dive In

If you are ready to embrace all that the Spirit has in store for you, then dive into his Word today. Devote yourself to studying more about the fruit of the Spirit. Find out God's character as it relates to the fruit. A good book for that is an old one called *The Knowledge of the Holy* by A. W. Tozer. You can read it for free on my website Godgirl.com. It's a part of the God Girl Academy 201. Come by and dive into more knowledge of the Holy Spirit and how he changes a life.

Ask Yourself

When you look at your life, how much of the fruit of the Spirit do you see? Circle all of the ones you have in your life most of the time: love, joy, peace, patience, kindness, goodness, faithfulness, gentleness, and self-control.

Now take a look at the fruit of the flesh and see how much of this there is in your life: selfishness, joylessness, conflict, impatience, mercilessness, immorality, unfaithfulness, pride, and self-indulgence.

If you want to trade the fruit of the flesh for the fruit of the Spirit, then commit your life anew to God today. Tell him that you are tired of responding to the flesh, and ask him to guide you with his Spirit.

Pray It

Dear God, please show me where I act on my flesh rather than trusting your Spirit. Give me more of you and less of me. Help me to feed the fruit of the Spirit to others and to give up my life for you. Amen.

Give It

As you finish this study, give the fruit of it away. Find at least two people in your life to tell about the fruit. Tell them something they may not have known. Offer them your own story; be transparent and let them know what God has done for you. Buy a book for them. Invite them to do this study with you. Pray for them, and feed them all of the fruit that God has provided in your life.

Dictionary

- **Day 4**

Love:

  a. An action, which sometimes comes with feelings, in which God's joy, peace, patience, kindness, goodness, faithfulness, gentleness, and self-control are seen in the way his children behave toward undeserving people

  b. A caring commitment, in which affection and delight are shown to others, which is grounded in the nature of God himself.[1]

  c. As a characteristic of the Christian life [love] is consequent upon God's unfathomable love and infinite mercy toward us.[2]

- **Day 7**

Joy: a gift of the Holy Spirit that allows you to celebrate the very character of God in easy as well as trying times of life

The opposite of joy: joylessness, doubt, fear, worry, and other results of the flesh fearing the very character of God in times of trial and testing

1. Martin H. Manser, Alister E. McGrath, J. I. Packer, and Donald J. Wiseman, eds., *Zondervan Dictionary of Bible Themes: The Accessible and Comprehensive Tool for Topical Studies* (Grand Rapids: Zondervan, 1999).
2. Timothy George, *Galatians*, The New American Commentary, vol. 30 (Nashville: Broadman & Holman Publishers, 1994), 400.

• Day 20

Goodness: whatever pleases God

• Day 25

Gentleness: a mildness and calmness in spirit that is teachable and humble toward God and others

• Day 26

Pride: thinking of yourself as the most important or deserving person in the world

Verse List

Day 2

Galatians 5:22–23—"But the fruit of the Spirit is love, joy, peace, patience, kindness, goodness, faithfulness, gentleness, self-control; against such things there is no law."

Galatians 3:3—"Are you so foolish? Having begun by the Spirit, are you now being perfected by the flesh?"

Philippians 1:6—"And I am sure of this, that he who began a good work in you will bring it to completion at the day of Jesus Christ."

Romans 7:4—"Likewise, my brothers, you also have died to the law through the body of Christ, so that you may belong to another, to him who has been raised from the dead, in order that we may bear fruit for God."

Day 3

1 Corinthians 12:7—"To each is given the manifestation of the Spirit for the common good."

John 15:4–5—"Abide in me, and I in you. As the branch cannot bear fruit by itself, unless it abides in the vine, neither can you, unless you abide in me. I am the vine; you are the branches. Whoever abides in me and I in him, he it is that bears much fruit, for apart from me you can do nothing."

Luke 6:43–44—"For no good tree bears bad fruit, nor again does a bad tree bear good fruit, for each tree is known by its own fruit. For figs are not gathered from thornbushes, nor are grapes picked from a bramble bush."

Matthew 3:10—"Even now the axe is laid to the root of the trees. Every tree therefore that does not bear good fruit is cut down and thrown into the fire."

• Day 4

Luke 6:27–28—"But I say to you who hear, Love your enemies, do good to those who hate you, bless those who curse you, pray for those who abuse you."

Luke 10:27—"And he answered, 'You shall love the Lord your God with all your heart and with all your soul and with all your strength and with all your mind, and your neighbor as yourself.'"

John 13:35—"By this all people will know that you are my disciples, if you have love for one another."

Ephesians 2:4–5—"But God, being rich in mercy, because of the great love with which he loved us, even when we were dead in our trespasses, made us alive together with Christ—by grace you have been saved."

Ephesians 5:1–2—"Therefore be imitators of God, as beloved children. And walk in love, as Christ loved us and gave himself up for us, a fragrant offering and sacrifice to God."

1 John 4:7–8—"Beloved, let us love one another, for love is from God, and whoever loves has been born of God and knows God. Anyone who does not love does not know God, because God is love."

• Day 8

Philippians 4:8—"Finally, brothers, whatever is true, whatever is honorable, whatever is just, whatever is pure, whatever is lovely, whatever is commendable, if there is any excellence, if there is anything worthy of praise, think about these things."

• Day 9

Resentment

Isaiah 45:9—"Woe to him who strives with him who formed him, a pot among earthen pots! Does the clay say to him who forms it, 'What are you making?' or 'Your work has no handles?'"

Bitterness

Ephesians 4:31—"Let all bitterness and wrath and anger and clamor and slander be put away from you, along with all malice."

Hebrews 12:15—"See to it that no one fails to obtain the grace of God; that no 'root of bitterness' springs up and causes trouble, and by it many become defiled."

Jealousy/Discontentment

Proverbs 14:30—"A tranquil heart gives life to the flesh, but envy makes the bones rot."

Galatians 5:19–21—"Now the works of the flesh are evident: sexual immorality, impurity, sensuality, idolatry, sorcery, enmity, strife, jealousy, fits of anger, rivalries, dissensions, divisions, envy, drunkenness, orgies, and things like these. I warn you, as I warned you before, that those who do such things will not inherit the kingdom of God."

Philippians 4:11–13—"Not that I am speaking of being in need, for I have learned in whatever situation I am to be content. I know how to be brought low, and I know how to abound. In any and every circumstance, I have learned the secret of facing plenty and hunger, abundance and need. I can do all things through him who strengthens me."

1 Timothy 6:6—"But godliness with contentment is great gain."

Day 10

1 John 1:9—"If we confess our sins, he is faithful and just to forgive us our sins and to cleanse us from all unrighteousness."

Romans 8:1—"There is therefore now no condemnation for those who are in Christ Jesus."

Psalm 32:5—"I acknowledged my sin to you, and I did not cover my iniquity; I said, 'I will confess my transgressions to the Lord,' and you forgave the iniquity of my sin."

Proverbs 28:13—"Whoever conceals his transgressions will not prosper, but he who confesses and forsakes them will obtain mercy."

Day 11

Luke 6:36—"Be merciful, even as your Father is merciful."

Psalm 57:10—"For your steadfast love is great to the heavens, your faithfulness to the clouds."

Lamentations 3:22–24—"The steadfast love of the Lord never ceases; his mercies never come to an end; they are new every morning; great is your faithfulness."

Day 13

Romans 8:25—"But if we hope for what we do not see, we wait for it with patience."

2 Timothy 2:24—"And the Lord's servant must not be quarrelsome but kind to everyone, able to teach, patiently enduring evil."

1 Thessalonians 5:14—"And we urge you, brothers, admonish the idle, encourage the fainthearted, help the weak, be patient with them all."

Day 26

Matthew 23:12—"Whoever exalts himself will be humbled, and whoever humbles himself will be exalted."

Proverbs 11:2—"When pride comes, then comes disgrace, but with the humble is wisdom."

James 4:6—"But he gives more grace. Therefore it says, "God opposes the proud, but gives grace to the humble."

Day 27

Matthew 5:5—"Blessed are the meek, for they shall inherit the earth."

Colossians 3:12—"Put on then, as God's chosen ones, holy and beloved, compassionate hearts, kindness, humility, meekness, and patience."

James 3:13—"Who is wise and understanding among you? By his good conduct let him show his works in the meekness of wisdom."

• Day 28

Matthew 10:38–39—"And whoever does not take his cross and follow me is not worthy of me. Whoever finds his life will lose it, and whoever loses his life for my sake will find it."

Matthew 20:16—"So the last will be first, and the first last."

Luke 14:27—"Whoever does not bear his own cross and come after me cannot be my disciple."

Hayley DiMarco is the bestselling and award-winning author of over thirty books, including *Mean Girls, God Girl,* and *Devotions for the God Girl.* Hayley mentors young women at GodGirl.com, and she and her husband, Michael, run their publishing company, Hungry Planet (www.hungryplanet.net), just outside of Nashville, Tennessee.

Become the Woman God Created You to Be

When you become a God Girl, your life will never be the same.

Available Wherever Books Are Sold